ENDOR

G.A.L.S. must certainly be one of the gems in God's Jewelry Box! I have known several of them for many years and know for a fact that their lives reflect God's love in moments of crisis as well as the more tranquil times in life. From the very beginning of this ministry, their heart's desire has been to convey the precious gift of salvation (the most precious jewel of all) to every individual they meet. Personally, they inspire me with their creativity, passion, and joy. Professionally, they add pearls of wisdom and facets of truth during every presentation, whether to a group of 10 or 300. My prayer is that you will uncover the new and deeper treasure of God's love for you, His precious jewel, in every chapter of this book.

Kay Doyle
Chief Administrative Officer, Cornerstone Assistance Network

Carolyn, Marilyn, Sharon, Linda, and Terri are wonderful ladies who have a genuine love for Christ. Their work is a good introduction both to their devotion to the Lord as well as the Scripture itself. The value of their book is also an encouragement to ladies to practically live out our faith in Christ. I encourage you to get to know this group God's Amazing Love Storytellers.

Dr. Scott Maze
Senior Pastor, North Richland Hills Baptist Church/Cross Church

Read this book to experience the journey of faith and love that the G.A.L.S. have embarked on! They have spoken at our United Methodist Women's group several times and each time, the joy of their faith shines brighter than any jewel. They have inspired many with their books and this book is no exception. It is another step on their chosen path of spreading God's love. Read and enjoy.

Maryanne Hollifield
Teacher, St. Luke United Methodist Church Haltom City

I have had the pleasure of seeing the G.A.L.S. perform many times and I cannot say enough good things about them. They truly bring something unique, exciting, uplifting, and invigorating to the atmosphere. They empower my faith and they leave me wanting more. Even their cookbooks have nuggets of Scripture and inspirational messages added to the recipes. In fact, I see the G.A.L.S. like cake. Each ingredient has its own uniqueness, flavor, and purpose on its own, but when you mix all the ingredients together, something magical happens. The end result is fantastic and the flavor is exquisite! These ladies are charming, funny, talented, and creative and they not only know how to mix the cake batter, they will also stir up your love for the Lord!

Officer Brian McClenny
Clergy And Police Alliance Coordinator, C.A.P.A.

I have known most of the G.A.L.S. for many years and observed their Christ-led ministry of amazing storytelling. They utilize their insightful, God-given talents to communicate the multifaceted gems of who God is and the rich blessings He has for all who will follow Him. In each chapter of this book, the G.A.L.S. share their life-narratives in such a way as to intimately connect the reader with God. The following words from Chapter 4 spoke to me about living life with purpose, "If you want to invest in something that will never tarnish, share the good news with as many people as you can."

<u>God's Jewelry Box</u> shares God's Good News and will serve as tarnish remover for your life as you are inspired, strengthened, and encouraged to walk daily with him. Wonderful stories about jewelry and Jesus, what could be better!

Aundrea Campbell
Ministry to Music, Children /Women/Springdale Baptist Church

While reading God's Jewelry Box authored by the G.A.L.S., the stories compiled by each of these authors brought to remembrance my own special treasures in my jewelry box. Some I bought, others were inherited each having a special memory. These stories linked to various Scriptures that aptly attributes to our faith, life circumstances, and encouragement for daily living.

As I journeyed through the stories, I found myself connecting to each piece of jewelry in my own jewelry box. I am reminded of the Scripture in *Malachi 3:17* which says, *"They will be mine, says the Lord of Hosts" a special possession (jewel, treasure) on the day I am preparing..."* (Holman). I highly recommend these "special treasures" in story form for those desiring to be inspired to be one of God's jewels.

Vonnie Kohn
Artist, Founder-National Association of Christian Prophetic Artists

G.A.L.S. have beautifully woven practical stories of their own lives with spiritual truths. This is an amazing book and devotional. I highly recommend this book to anyone wanting to get closer to God.

Tim Shields
President, Christian Media Association

God's Jewelry Box is just one more way the G.A.L.S. illuminate the truth of God's amazing love. From the first time I met these women, I knew that their creativity was a gift from God that pointed to a holy and righteous Savior. The gems of truth gleaned from their short stories will empower you to dig deeper into God's Word and lead you to the greatest treasure of all, His son Jesus Christ. Prepare to be dazzled as you dig through each chapter for treasures and jewels of God's unfailing love.

Delaine Godwin
Moderator, Presbyterian Women at Ridglea Presbyterian Church

God's Jewelry Box

by God's Amazing Love Storytellers

Sharon Booker
Carolyn Hedgecock
Terri Howell
Linda Patterson
Marilyn Phillips

Copyright © 2018 by God's Amazing Love Storytellers

All rights reserved.

Sharon Booker, Carolyn Hedgecock,

Terri Howell, Linda Patterson, and Marilyn Phillips,

retain copyright on their own articles.

Some Scripture quotations are from the
New King James Version®.
Copyright © 1982 by Thomas Nelson.
Used by permission. All rights reserved.

Some Scripture quotations are from
THE HOLY BIBLE,
NEW INTERNATIONAL VERSION®, NIV®
Copyright© 1973, 1978, 1984, 2011 by Biblica, Inc.™
Used by permission. All rights reserved worldwide

The logo for G.A.L.S. was designed by Dianna Lago.

Visit http://www.GodsAmazingLoveStorytellers.com

for information about

God's Amazing Love Storytellers

storytellergals@gmail.com

TABLE OF CONTENTS

Introduction: How to Use this Book..................................... 8
1. To Share About God's Greatest Treasures................ 11
   The Price of Pearls – *Carolyn*................................... 12
   The Gold Medal – *Sharon*... 14
   The Treasure Box – *Linda*.. 16
   Secret Jewelry Box – *Carolyn*.................................. 18
2. To Remind Me to Pray.. 21
   In God We Trust – *Marilyn*....................................... 22
   Jewels of Prayer – *Sharon*.. 24
   India Beads – *Marilyn*.. 26
   Teardrop Necklace – *Linda*...................................... 28
3. To Share and Claim God's Promises......................... 31
   The Eagles – *Linda*... 32
   God Keeps Promises – *Marilyn*............................... 34
   Forgotten Necklace – *Carolyn*.................................. 36
   Precious Friend – *Linda*... 39
   Engraved – *Marilyn*... 42
   The Missing Stone – *Carolyn*.................................. 44
4. To Teach About Heaven.. 47
   Crowns – *Marilyn*.. 48
   Gates of Pearls – *Carolyn*.. 50
   Pearls and the Purple Pendant – *Terri*..................... 52
   Tarnished by Time – *Carolyn*................................... 54
5. To Help Others Understand New Life in Christ......... 57
   Pure Heart – *Linda*... 58
   Cross Collection – *Marilyn*...................................... 60
6. To See God's Care During Difficult Times................ 63
   Cancer – *Marilyn*... 64
   Jewelry's Melody – *Linda*.. 66
   Cystic Fibrosis – *Marilyn*.. 68
   Worry Doll – *Carolyn*... 70
   Butterfly Promises – *Marilyn*................................... 72

Pure Love – *Linda*...	74
Perfect Plan – *Carolyn*...	76
Always There – *Carolyn*.......................................	78
Noises of Life – *Terri*...	79
7. To Remember Covenant Relationships...................	**83**
Wedding Band – *Marilyn*......................................	84
The Silver Tie – *Terri*...	86
My Beloved – *Carolyn*	88
8. To Pass Along a Godly Legacy.................................	**91**
Roots – *Terri*...	92
Daddy's Ring – *Linda*...	94
A Good Name – *Carolyn*.......................................	96
Floral Brooch – *Sharon*...	98
9. To Know my Identity in Christ...............................	**101**
The Purple Cord – *Terri*..	102
Your Name – *Marilyn*...	104
Rings of Deception – *Sharon*................................	106
10. To Teach About Stewardship.................................	**109**
Simple Pin – *Sharon*...	110
My Dad's Necklace – *Carolyn*...............................	112
A Tangled Mess – *Sharon*.....................................	114
11. To Focus on Spiritual Matters and Truth...............	**117**
Fruity, Fun Earrings – *Terri*...................................	118
The Lens – *Sharon*..	120
Mother's Pearls – *Linda*..	122
Special Design – *Marilyn*......................................	124
Trinkets – *Sharon*...	126
Dressed Appropriately – *Marilyn*..........................	129
Surprised – *Carolyn*..	132
Charmed – *Sharon*..	134
12. To Teach About True Wealth.................................	**137**
Mom's Love Notes – *Marilyn*................................	138
Triangle of Rubies and Pearls – *Terri*....................	140
Rich – *Carolyn*...	142

Gramma Treasures – *Linda*...	144
13. To Use During Spiritual Battles................................	147
Mighty Warrior – *Carolyn*..	148
Three Strands Strong – *Terri*..	150
Angels All Around – *G.A.L.S.*......................................	152
14. To Ask God to Order My Steps.................................	155
Flip Flops – *Carolyn*..	156
Watches and Time – *Sharon*...	158
Cut and Molded – *Terri*...	160
15. To Build Up Faith in Believers.................................	163
Faith, Hope, Love – *Marilyn*..	164
Quick Fix – *Carolyn*..	166
Trumpet – *Linda*..	168
16. To Explore the Power of Praise................................	171
Lead Me to the Rock – *Sharon*.....................................	172
A New Song – *Terri*..	174
Jesus is the Reason – *Marilyn*......................................	176
17. To Open Doors to Share God's Love..........................	179
Duel Blessing – *Linda*..	180
Ten Commandments – *Marilyn*.....................................	182
Charm Bracelet – *Linda*..	184
Yellow Rose – *Terri*..	186
Drama, Drama, Drama – *Linda*....................................	188
Witness Bracelets – *G.A.L.S.*......................................	190
God's Amazing Love Storytellers.....................................	195
G.A.L.S. Bios and Contact Information.............................	196
The Jewels of Heaven..	198
Evangelism Partners International (E.P.I.).........................	202
G.A.L.S. Photos...	204

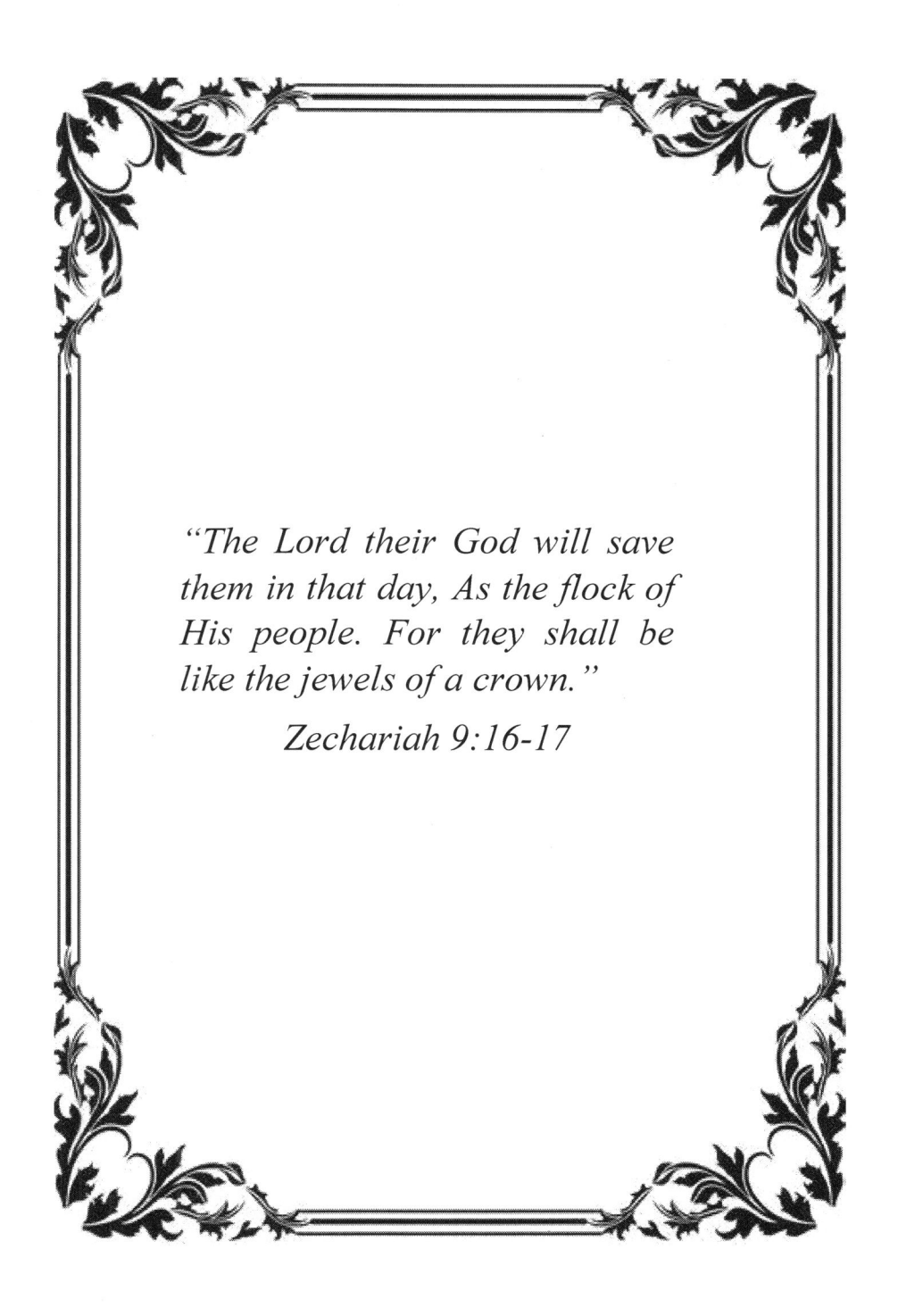

"The Lord their God will save them in that day, As the flock of His people. For they shall be like the jewels of a crown."

Zechariah 9:16-17

Introduction: How to use this Book

The G.A.L.S. love our jewelry and bling. God must love jewels too; after all, He created them. The KJV Bible has an amazing 1,704 references to gemstones and jewels. Treasures can be found in 72 verses and 24 verses speak directly about jewelry. God even refers to His people as jewels in a crown that sparkles.

When we get to heaven, we are going to see treasures unlike anything on earth. Just try to picture with us the breathtaking beauty of the throne room. Revelation 4:3 describes the one sitting on the throne as similar to a jasper stone, a crystal, and a sardius, red in color surrounded by a rainbow with an emerald.

We wonder if we will see the breastplates the priests wore in Exodus. They contained emerald, topaz, sardius, diamond, sapphire, turquoise, amethyst, agate, jacinth, jasper, onyx, and beryl. Revelation 21:20 speaks of layers upon layers of jewels far beyond human comprehension.

The G.A.L.S. began thinking about the implications and connections between items found in our jewelry boxes and the Word of God.

Overwhelmed with excitement, like the energizer bunny, we didn't want to stop. Stories began to flow out of us like the wind of the Holy Spirit at Pentecost.

We couldn't believe how quickly our stories came. Soon, we realized this would be more than one book. What a fun and personal way to have a series of books useful for: quiet times, family devotions, and perfect for Girls' Nights Out.

Because our own personal stories flowed so effortlessly, we wanted others to have a place to keep stories of their family treasures. That was the beginning of a separate journal called <u>What's In Your Jewelry Box?</u> We saw the possibility of using <u>God's Jewelry Box</u> and <u>Jewelry Gem Bible Study and Leader Guide</u> for conferences, Bible studies, and retreats.

With full joy, we have shared some of our favorite stories and applications between our jewelry and the Biblical truths hidden inside each piece. It is our desire to encourage you to search inside your jewelry box and find your own special stories with spiritual lessons you can share with your friends and family.

To get started, use the journal space provided in this book to answer some thought-provoking questions. We pray you will find the presence of God in everyday ordinary items so you can discover God's will, truth, and purpose for your life. Scripture is also included to help in your quest. Beloved friends, may we each become priceless jewels that sparkle in the crown of the King.

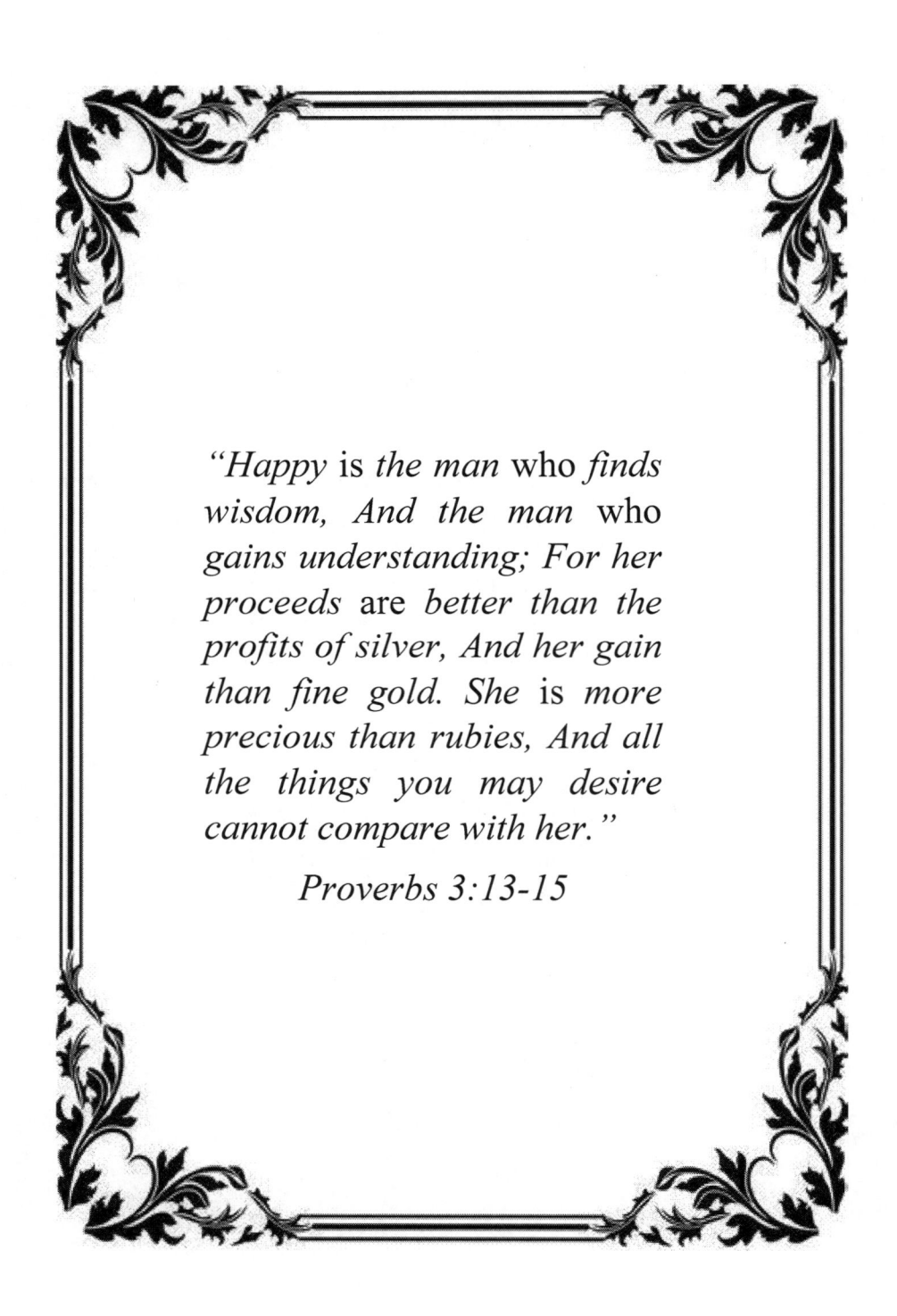

"Happy is *the man* who *finds wisdom, And the man* who *gains understanding; For her proceeds* are *better than the profits of silver, And her gain than fine gold. She* is *more precious than rubies, And all the things you may desire cannot compare with her."*

Proverbs 3:13-15

Chapter 1

To Share About God's Greatest Treasures

"Do not lay up for yourselves treasures on earth, where moth and rust destroy and where thieves break in and steal; but lay up for yourselves treasures in heaven, where neither moth nor rust destroys and where thieves do not break in and steal. For where your treasure is, there your heart will be also."

Matthew 6:19-21

The Price of Pearls

My Uncle Buster was a family favorite. What a pearl of a guy! If anyone asked my uncle if he wanted to go anywhere, the answer was always, "Yes." At the age of ninety, he moved into an assisted living home in Nashville, Tennessee, but that didn't slow him down. It was cute because Uncle Buster always had a girlfriend and was a sought-after dinner date for many widows in the facility. However, his one true love was his deceased wife, Aunt Cora.

Totally devoted to one another, Uncle Buster and Aunt Cora never had any children. My mother was one of his favorite nieces, and she inherited Aunt Cora's beautiful pearl anniversary ring. Set in a 14K gold setting, two perfect pearls rest next to each other with little diamonds on either side. The ring symbolized their close happy marriage. Mother gave me the ring to make sure it, and the story behind it, stays in our family.

How pearls are formed is a fascinating story. A pearl is the only jewel that is produced by requiring an oyster to give its life. Here's what happens. A small grain of sand slips inside an oyster's shell. It is a painful irritant to the sea creature, so an oyster secretes a substance over the intruder to help ease the pain. The process continues until a pearl is formed inside the soft and pliable surface. An oyster dies once the shell is opened and the pearl is revealed.

Pearls from oysters are God's way of showing us that we will have difficulties in our lives. When we effectively deal with hardships, we, like pearls, can grow into beautiful jewels. Learning to overcome obstacles helps us identify with others who are going through similar painful circumstances.

When we learn to not focus on the irritations of life, then we can become gorgeous treasures full of patience, humility, mercy, perseverance, and discernment. A paradox, we must lose our lives in order to find them.

✝ Carolyn

Jewelry Gems

"Again, the kingdom of heaven is like a merchant seeking beautiful pearls, who when had found one pearl of great price, went and sold all that he had and bought it."
Matthew 13:45-46

1. How are God's righteous children like jewels? Explain *Matthew 13:45-46* in your own words. _____

_____

_____

_____

_____

2. Write about a painful experience that taught you valuable life lessons which helped turn you into a pearl. _____

_____

_____

_____

_____

The Gold Medal

I love the Olympics! I enjoyed watching the competitions and hearing the Olympians' stories. All the training and sacrifice came together in that final moment of competition. Extraordinarily outstanding athletes were awarded gold medals. A coveted medallion of sterling silver plated in six grams of real gold is worth about $600.00, but is invaluable to the winner.

Tucked away in a metal container inside a drawer of my jewelry box, I stumbled upon my gold medal. An intercollegiate tournament trophy from my freshman year of college for table tennis was found. Not the illustrious reward of true Olympians, it is certainly of less significance and value. The Apostle Paul coaches us to be spiritual Olympians. He admonishes believers to be faithful to some basic spiritual calisthenics:

- *"Discipline my body and bring it into subjection." I Corinthians 9:27*
- *"Present your body as a living sacrifice." Romans 12:1*
- Throw off everything that hinders and trips you up; persevere and run the race God has marked off for you. *Hebrews 12:1*
- Forget what's behind and *"I press toward the goal for the prize of the upward call of God in Christ Jesus." Philippians 3:13-14*
- Run in such a way as to get the prize. *I Corinthians 9:24*

The Scriptures point us to an award that is far more precious than a gold medallion. The reward awaiting Christ followers is a crown of life. Unlike the medal in which the Olympians hang around their necks, the saints will be casting down their crowns before the heavenly podium on which the King of kings and Lord of lords sits enthroned.

✝ Sharon

Jewelry Gems

"The twenty-four elders fall down before Him who sits on the throne and worship Him who lives forever and ever, and cast their crowns before the throne, Saying "You are worthy, Oh LORD, To receive glory and honor and power; For You created all things, And by Your will they exist and were created."
Revelation 4:10-11

1. Describe a time in your life when you experienced the euphoric feeling of victory. _____

_____

_____

_____

2. List practical things you need to change to be better prepared to effectively run your spiritual race. _____

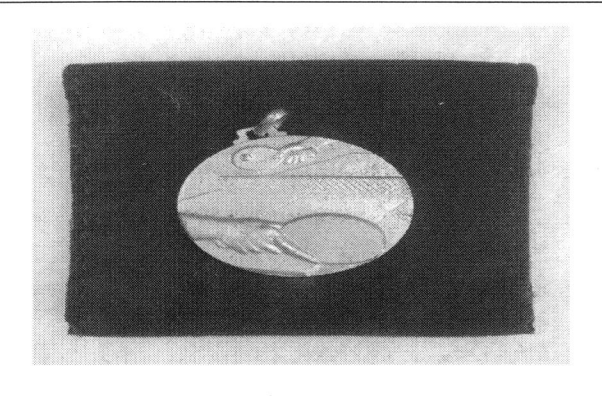

_____

_____

_____

_____

The Treasure Box

From the top shelf of my closet, I pulled down a small box to see what was inside. To my extreme delight, it was "The Treasure Box!" Inside was my parents' jewelry. With six girls to share their heirlooms, this was my stash.

My mother loved the color red. It was evident as you looked at her wardrobe, etc. When I found her ruby earrings, I could "see her" wearing them with a frilly red dress headed out to church.

Mother was an intercessor for the local Christian T.V. station. She went by the name of "Joy," which fit her perfectly. Mom had a cheerful disposition and was known for her beautiful smile. In her younger years, she was the first Redbud Queen in the state of Oklahoma. Inside and out, Mom was truly beautiful.

When Mom was 84, she went to heaven. I miss her. My first best friend, I remember us sitting on the bed in the back bedroom of our single-wide mobile home. She would wax the hallway, the length of the house, and sit on the bed with my siblings and me as it dried. Mom would make up stories with each of us being the "star" character. We would sing songs and laugh. In those early years, we moved frequently due to my daddy's job. Mother was the thread that kept us on track throughout our many moves and many schools. After my sister and I left home, Mother focused her attention more on the Lord and my daddy.

All of us need someone to keep us on track when we "grow up" and leave the nest. We realize it is our turn to nurture and teach our children. Mother had found the red thread of redemption our Father God provided from Genesis to Revelation through the blood of Jesus Christ, our Redeemer. Jesus sent the Holy Spirit to earth to teach us. My family grew in knowledge of the Kingdom of God. He now fills our lives with purpose, adventure, and the message of hope for mankind.

♪Linda

Jewelry Gems

"In Him we have redemption through His blood, the forgiveness of sins, according to the riches of His grace."
Ephesians 1:7

1. Describe how you see the red thread of redemption in the Bible.

_____

_____

_____

_____

2. Make a list of people who need God in their lives. Write a prayer for each person. Record the dates of each prayer for specific lost people on your list. _____

_____

_____

_____

_____

Secret Jewelry Box

"He who dwells in the secret place of the Most High shall abide under the shadow of the Almighty. I will say of the LORD, "He is my refuge and fortress; My God, in Him I will trust."
Psalm 91:1-2

With nothing but happy memories, I remember sitting at what my grandmother called her "primping table." Consisting of a large mirror, attached to a desk with two drawers on either side, it was where Grandmother kept her jewelry and put on her make-up. The coolest part of her vanity table was the hidden compartment. She hired someone to shorten one of the drawers and build a secret cubicle behind the drawer which held a small wooden container. In her secret treasure box, she kept money and her heirloom jewelry. After my grandmother went to heaven, I inherited her vanity with the compartment.

It took me a while to want to open the special container because it would be to admit my grandmother was gone. Now, over twenty years later, it is still hard for me to do. However, one of my most treasured finds in her box was a ring with two opals and two rubies. I don't know what the center stone looked like because it is missing.

Unfortunately, the ring was worn so much that the back part of it was gone. I think the ring must have belonged to my great-grandmother or even my great-great grandmother. Regardless, who it belonged to, I couldn't bear to throw the ring away or wear it … until one day, I got an idea.

I decided to take the ring and turn it into a necklace. At the time, my kids were little, and I didn't have the money to take the ring to a jeweler. So, I got some fabric, ribbon, lace, and buttons from my grandmother's button box and began designing. I ended up with a fan necklace.

After I made this one-of-a-kind necklace, I enjoyed wearing it quite a lot, but to be honest, it's been years since I last wore it. Now, I have it hanging on a jewelry rack in my closet, along with other discards. When I saw it last night, it was like running into an old nearly-forgotten friend. It's out of style, but I'm going to wear it today. It holds memories and many secrets.

Did you know that God has a secret place He has designed for you, His beloved? You can't book a vacation there. It can only be found by spending time with the Lord and dwelling with Him. Let me tell you, it is a rare find ... a fortress in times of trouble and a shelter from the storms of life. Get to know the Savior, and I promise you, it will be the greatest treasure you will ever discover on this earth.

✞ Carolyn

Jewelry Gems

1. Do you have a secret compartment where you hide things that are special to you? Where is it? Why did you choose to hide things there? If you don't have any hiding places, think about where a good place might be and write about it. _____

_____

_____

_____

_____

_____

_____

_____

2. Read *Psalm 91:1-2* and write in your own words what it means to you. _____

_____

_____

_____

_____

_____

_____

_____

Chapter 2

To Remind Me to Pray

"Therefore I say to you, whatever things you ask when you pray, believe that you receive them, and you will have them."

Mark 11:24

In God We Trust

American history demonstrates that our nation was founded on Christian principles. The founding fathers openly prayed and acknowledged that God answers prayers for a nation when people earnestly seek Him.

Our money even represents our nations' belief. The first time "In God We Trust" appeared on our coins was in 1864 on the two cent coin. By 1909, it was included on most of the other coins. A law approved by President Dwight Eisenhower on July 30, 1956, declared "In God We Trust" as our nation's motto and must appear on American currency.

I'm thankful for our founding fathers and the sacrifices made for freedom. When I hear the song, *"God Bless America,"* it makes me weep because so many nations can't sing this song.

It is with great pride that I wear patriotic jewelry and share about the freedom of religion that Americans are able to enjoy. We can put our trust in God. He hears our prayers.

✝ Marilyn

Jewelry Gems

"If My people who are called by My name will humble themselves, and pray and seek My face, and turn from their wicked ways, then I will hear from heaven, and will forgive their sin and heal their land."
                    II Chronicles 7:14-16

1. What does "In God We Trust" mean to you? _____

_____

_____

_____

_____

2. Write a prayer for our country. Stop and pray for our country and those in authority._____

_____

_____

_____

_____

_____

Jewels of Prayer

My present jewelry box is a former card catalog from the library in which I served for 24 years. Every drawer is full of something: earrings, bracelets, necklaces, rings, and a plethora of other things harboring great memories.

Some days, I open a drawer to take out a piece of jewelry and instead I am drawn into a memory as vivid as the day it happened. A familiar face of the past will form in my mind: a student, a teacher, a parent or any number of other people. Each person is one of God's jewels created for His glory. It is then that I understand He is inviting me to stand in the gap for them in prayer.

As a watchman on God's wall, the work is never done. The past cannot be changed, but people have a destiny that can be affected by my prayers.

☦ Sharon

Jewelry Gems

"So I sought for a man among them who would make a wall, and stand in the gap before Me on behalf of the land, that I should not destroy it; but I found no one."
Ezekiel 22:30

1. People in our past deeply affect our lives. Praying for them changes you and creates opportunity for God to do an amazing work in their lives. Who are the people from your past for whom God would have you pray? List their names and date your prayer request.

_____

_____

_____

_____

_____

2. Ask God to show you how you can impact a life from your past with a blessing from the present. How can you be a faithful watchman on the wall? Take action and begin today!

_____

_____

_____

_____

_____

_____

India Beads

Moi and her husband, Dr. (Thang) Langkhanghang Lianzaw, were in America for over eight years. They studied at and graduated from Southwestern Baptist Theological Seminary. Thang received a Doctorate degree. Moi received a Masters. They were members of our church where my husband, Nolan, taught a Sunday School class for adults that they attended. We became close friends!

In fact, Moi and I wrote a book, *Called From the Dust: A Journey of Faith, Hope and Love*, about their call to ministry. Moi and Thang returned to India after receiving degrees.

Thang has a ministry where he and his team go to remote villages to share about Jesus. At times, they are met with hostility. Their team was severely beaten and put in jail at one village.

My friends gave me a handmade necklace of tiny beads from India. It reminds me to pray for them and the urgency to share about Jesus to those who are lost. They may not be in a remote village; but might live right next door.

✝ Marilyn

Jewelry Gems

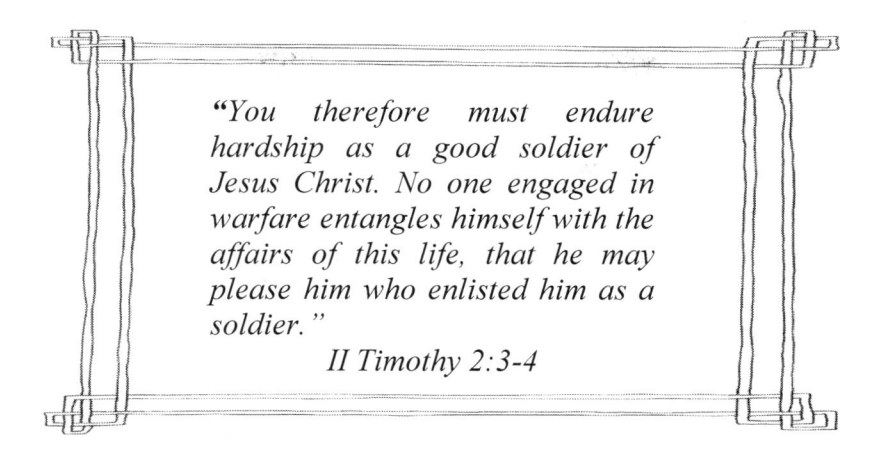

"You therefore must endure hardship as a good soldier of Jesus Christ. No one engaged in warfare entangles himself with the affairs of this life, that he may please him who enlisted him as a soldier."
II Timothy 2:3-4

1. Have you ever wanted to be a missionary or go on a mission trip? How can you be a missionary where you live? If so, write about it. _____

_____

_____

_____

_____

2. How can you be a soldier for Christ? _____

_____

_____

_____

_____

_____

_____

Teardrop Necklace

Our God is always looking for humble intercessors. He loves us all so very much. Yet, even though He's made a way for us to be with Him for all eternity, there are those who don't understand and reject God.

Our Father sent the Holy Spirit to us after Jesus' resurrection. He is the Comforter, who will teach us all things, including how to intercede for others. We have examples in the Bible of those who knelt before the Lord in prayer and received answers, even miracles. The prophet, Daniel comes to mind first.

There is a delicate teardrop necklace that is hanging from a jewelry tree on my vanity. The pretty gold chain is not the original chain. It has been worn so often over time that it needed to be replaced. The teardrop pendant shows no wear. Tears are a cleansing force. They remind me of times spent in intense prayer. Scripture carries the promise that after tears, there comes a time of joy. We will be able to rejoice over those who respond to our Savior, Jesus Christ.

♪Linda

Jewelry Gems

"He who continually goes forth weeping, Bearing seed for sowing, Shall doubtless come again with rejoicing, Bringing his sheaves with him."
　　　　　　　　Psalm 126:6

1. Write about a time that someone told you they had been praying for you. How did that make you feel? _____

_____

_____

_____

_____

_____

2. What does it mean to intercede for someone? Would you be willing to join the Lord's army of intercessors? _____

_____

_____

_____

_____

_____

_____

_____

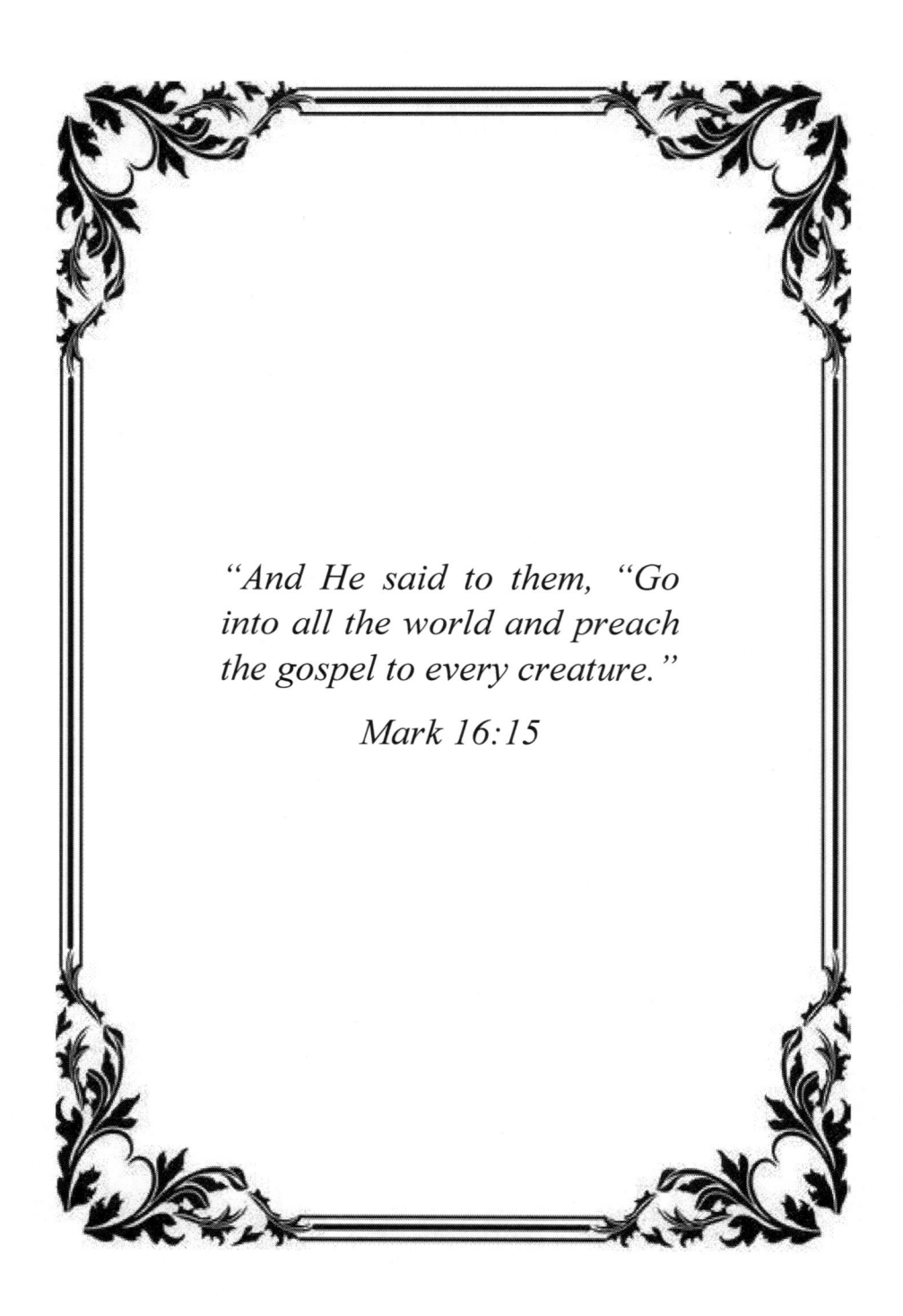

"And He said to them, "Go into all the world and preach the gospel to every creature."

Mark 16:15

Chapter 3

To Share and Claim God's Promises

"For all the promises of God in Him are Yes, and in Him Amen, to the glory of God through us."

II Corinthians 1:20

The Eagles

If you go to Albuquerque, New Mexico, you won't want to miss visiting Old Town. Gifted craftsmen of various cultures spread their beautiful jewelry and pottery along the sidewalks in front of the stores on the square. Assorted stones are used in their jewelry; however, the turquoise stone is the one that would consistently catch my daddy's eye.

Dad was a generous man who would buy us whatever we wanted, within reason. We would watch for what Daddy liked and get it for him for special occasions. The eagle was his favorite. Dad proudly wore his turquoise eagle belt buckles.

My hero was a WWII marine veteran. He worked in radar when it was new. Riding in the planes, he sometimes had to take over the tail-gunner's position. Once, Dad told me that after landing, he could not put his hand on any place that didn't have a bullet hole in it.

Eagles fly high and alone. What a powerful and majestic sight! I think that may be what Daddy admired. Being a Christian, he knew the Word and would want you to trust God's promises as he did.

♪Linda

Jewelry Gems

"But those who wait on the LORD shall renew their strength; They shall mount up with wings like eagles, They shall run and not be weary, They shall walk and not faint."
Isaiah 40:31

1. Describe a piece of jewelry you have that draws your attention to the Lord, especially in difficult times. _____

_____

_____

_____

_____

_____

2. What does it mean to you to "wait upon the LORD?" How can you explain this truth to others? _____

_____

_____

_____

_____

_____

_____

_____

God Keeps Promises

I taught in a private Christian school for several years. One of my favorite Bible stories to tell my second grade students was about Noah in *Genesis 6*. He was a righteous man, but the earth was filled with corruption. God gave Noah detailed instructions to build an ark. Gathering his family and animals, they entered the ark as God instructed. Every living thing was destroyed that was not in the ark.

It rained for 40 days and nights. After the flood, Noah, his family, and the animals emerged from the ark. Afterwards, an altar was built to honor the Lord, and they worshiped Him. God promised He would never destroy the earth with a flood again. A rainbow in the sky symbolized the promise.

When I wear my "God Keeps His Promises" pin, I'm reminded of a gracious God who has promised believers good things. There are approximately 3,573 promises in the Bible to give hope for the future. God's promises are waiting to be claimed!

✝ Marilyn

Jewelry Gems

"Let us hold fast the confession of our hope without wavering, for He who promised is faithful."
Hebrews 10:23

1. How can you know and keep God's promises? _____

_____

_____

_____

_____

_____

2. Explain about a time in your life when you claimed a promise from God. How did God fulfill it? _____

_____

_____

_____

_____

_____

> *"And this is the promise that He has promised us—eternal life."*
> *I John 2:25*

Forgotten Necklace

"What do you want for your 16th birthday?" my mother asked me long ago.

"An add-a-pearl necklace," I replied with no hesitation. Remembering as if it was yesterday, not only did I want that necklace, I thought I *had* to have it. All the popular girls wore one; so of course, I needed an add-a-pearl necklace, too!

Totally excited, I received the necklace. Each pearl was real, though small and dainty. Important events marked a reason to add more pearls. I loved it, but one day, I stopped wearing the must-have necklace, and forgot all about it.

Until we began writing this book, I haven't thought about that special necklace. Many moons have passed and boo coos of jewelry have been acquired through the years to replace it. But just the remembrance ignited an overwhelming sense of urgency to find my forgotten necklace.

Panic rushed over me until my search ended. Found in a red plastic box with old cotton batting, underneath a bunch of towels in my bathroom was my beloved necklace. It was twisted and tangled in knots. Feeling so careless, I felt like apologizing to it for the neglect.

I began to wonder why I've opted for costume glitzy pearls instead of desiring the 14K real deal. Agitated with myself, I tried to untangle the delicate necklace. Working through the twisted knots was tedious and not fun. I guess that's why I abandoned it long ago. I realized it takes time to fix messes.

While working on my tangled necklace, I thought about David in the Bible. He got into so much trouble when he abandoned God and chose something that looked glitzier. After much heartache, he repented and asked God to restore the joy of his salvation.

My add-a-pearl necklace ordeal has a great take-away. Usually when people come to the Lord, there is great joy and excitement. Life happens and before they know it, their relationship with the Lord can become twisted and tangled. When days get busy and life moves fast, it's easy to abandon time with the Lord. That's when chaos comes to town.

Without intentional care, the delicate chain of my necklace knotted into an un-wearable jumbled piece of jewelry. Looking back at my life, I remember periods of time that resembled the necklace disaster. Only when I have returned to the Lord, with my brokenness, full of knots and twists, and repented, has my joy been restored.

☦ Carolyn

Jewelry Gems

1. Write about the beautiful "pearls" that God has added to the unique necklace of your life. _____

_____

_____

_____

_____

_____

2. Record some tangled messes you have made in your life. How did God untangle each event?_____

_____

_____

_____

_____

_____

> *"Restore to me the joy of Your salvation, and uphold me with Your generous spirit."*
>
> *Psalm 51:12*

Precious Friend

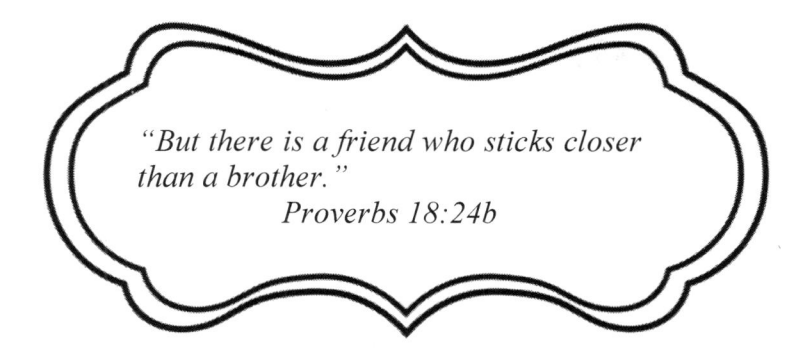

> *"But there is a friend who sticks closer than a brother."*
> Proverbs 18:24b

Hope, a beautiful lady at seventy-one years young, recently went to be with her Lord. The church was filled with friends and family who came to celebrate her life. She struggled with cancer, yet requested a big dance party for her seventieth birthday. Sure enough, she was dancing in the middle of a circle of loved ones who were spinning around with her.

In her seventieth year, Hope danced in the Christmas musical at our church. Dressed in Biblical attire, she joyfully worshipped the Lord with all her heart.

A few days before she left us, I brought my keyboard over, and Hope's daughters and I sang worship songs to/with her. Afterwards, she squeezed my hand gently as I told her we would soon dance together again.

One Sunday, Hope's daughters brought boxes into the hospitality room of our church. Their mother had told them that she wanted all her friends to have some of her jewelry. They invited the ladies to look through the bags and take whatever they wanted. There were necklaces of all colors, gems, and chain lengths.

Earrings, bracelets, and watches galore scattered over circular glass table tops. The admiring chatter over all the treasures filled the room. It was as though Hope was there with us. She would have loved that.

This piece of Christmas jewelry was one of my choices. The greatest treasure, however, is the loving memory of my friend, and sister in the Lord. God puts people in our lives as a representative of His love for us. We must always remember Jesus is the friend who sticks closer than a brother. In my case, closer than a sister.

♫Linda

Jewelry Gems

1. Describe a piece of jewelry that belonged to, or reminds you of a close friend.

2. What do you think about Hope's desire to share her jewelry with her friends?

Engraved

One Mother's Day, I received a gift from my husband with the names of our children engraved on it. Bryant, my son, was on the shape of a boy. Rebekah, my daughter, was on the shape of a girl. My initials were in the middle.

When I received the personalized necklace, tears of joy flowed! Many compliments were received each time it was worn. Rubbing my fingers over the boy and girl shapes, the inscriptions reminded me to pray for my children by name. Often, I would grasp the necklace and claim God's promises for each child.

How many times each day do you look at your hands? Each time, your palms should remind you to focus on God and His love for you. Memorize *Isaiah 49:16* and share the verse and meaning with others.

✞ Marilyn

Jewelry Gems

"See, I have engraved you on the palms of My hands; your walls are continually before Me."
Isaiah 49:16 NIV

1. Describe the jewelry you have that is engraved. If you don't have any, describe a piece you would like to have engraved. _____

_____

_____

_____

_____

_____

2. What does it mean that you are engraved on the palms of God's hands? How can you share this message? _____

_____

_____

_____

_____

_____

_____

_____

The Missing Stone

"I will seek what was lost and bring back what was driven away, bind up the broken and strengthen what was sick."
Ezekiel 34:16a

What a shame I thought when I picked up one of my favorite rings. Immediately, I noticed a little stone was missing. The ring was inexpensive, so to have it repaired would cost more than the original price.

For some reason, I can't part with my damaged ring. So pretty when I first bought it, I've enjoyed wearing it often. It's a mystery how or when the one small stone disappeared. The search for the small rhinestone has left me empty-handed every time I've looked for it.

I know I should probably throw it away, but I can't. Flawed beyond repair, I'll never feel comfortable wearing it again. Why do I keep it? I think I continue to hold on to it because I still have hope that the missing stone will someday be recovered.

There is also a spiritual connection I have to it. I am reminded of the parables of the missing coin, the missing sheep, and the prodigal son. The widow who lost her coin would not rest until she found it. Likewise, the shepherd, who had ninety-nine sheep in the fold was not content until his one lost sheep returned. The pinnacle story is about a rebellious son who left home and got involved with bad company. His father never stopped waiting and watching for his son's return. Life wasn't the same until the lost person, sheep, and coin were found. God is like that. He never gives up on anyone. No one is considered unredeemable. Jesus came to seek and to save the lost. If by chance you have a piece of jewelry with a missing stone, think back to the three parables and be reminded of God's promise in *Ezekiel 34:16*. He who promised is faithful!

☦ Carolyn

Jewelry Gems

1. Read *Ezekiel 34:16*. Make a list of people you know who are lost, or separated from loved ones, broken, weak, or sick. Write a prayer thanking God that He is more than able to repair every situation. Claim His promises and find Scriptures that give you hope while you wait.

2. Record days to pray for your loved ones and friends.

I have a friend who prays for people alphabetically. On Monday she prays for loved ones whose first names start with either "A," "B," or "C." On Tuesday, she prays for those whose first names range between "D" through "G." Wednesday is for loved ones from "H" to "K." Thursday she prays for those whose names range from "L" to "O." Friday she prays for people whose names begin with letters "P" to "S." Saturday she prays for those whose names begin with "T" through "Z." On Sunday, she prays for whomever the Lord lays on her mind. I like this system because it helps to remember to pray for everyone close to you. Devise a way you can remember to pray for your friends and love ones in the space below. Remember where there is much prayer, there is much power! _____

_____
_____
_____
_____
_____
_____
_____
_____
_____
_____
_____
_____

Chapter 4

To Teach About Heaven

"Jesus said to her, "I am the resurrection and the life. He who believes in Me, though he may die, he shall live."

John 11:25

Crowns

While searching through old pictures in my jewelry cabinet, I saw newspaper clippings and pictures from high school years. Memories flooded my mind. I had been a consistent winner of beauty contests. Each win, I received moments of glory with a sparkly tiara, huge trophy, and newspaper featured articles. Looking at my tiaras filled with sparkling rhinestones, I remember marveling at the beauty of each crown. The trophies and tiaras were displayed in prominent positions so they could easily be seen. The crowns and awards made me feel like I was beautiful and special.

One day, a fire in my apartment destroyed all furniture and precious possessions including the tiaras and trophies. Devastated by the lost, I felt empty without my trophies and crowns. Now, newspaper articles and pictures are all I have left. They are kept in my jewelry cabinet.

Through the years, God helped me focus on Bible truths. Now, I have discovered a new perspective. Searching through the Bible, I understood the trophies worth seeking are eternal, and we have the promise to receive the crown of life. Could there be anything better?

✝ Marilyn

Jewelry Gems

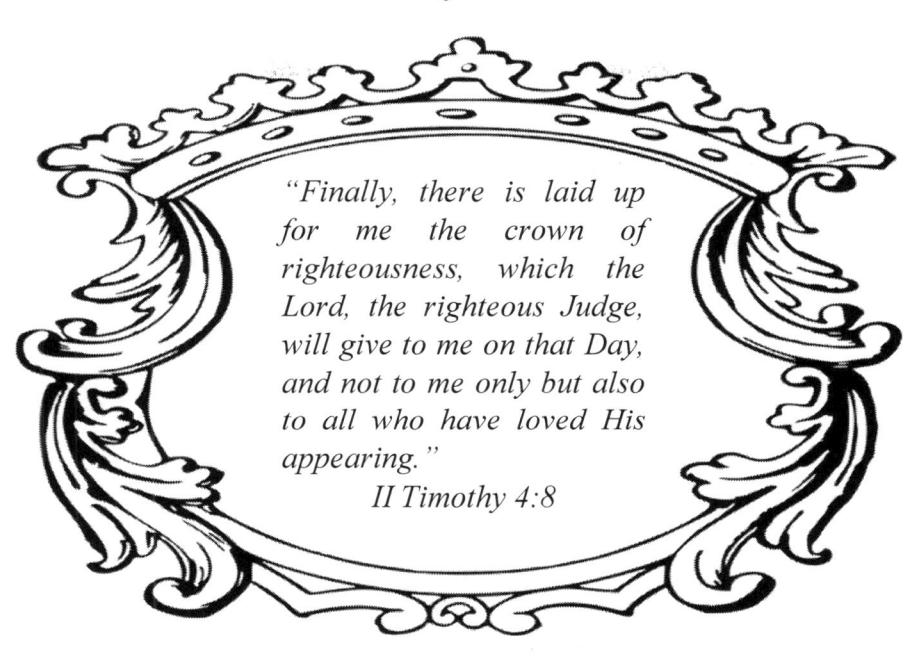

"Finally, there is laid up for me the crown of righteousness, which the Lord, the righteous Judge, will give to me on that Day, and not to me only but also to all who have loved His appearing."
II Timothy 4:8

1. What trophies or possessions do you have in your life that make you feel special? _____

_____

_____

_____

2. How can you receive the "crown of righteousness?" _____

_____

_____

_____

_____

Gates of Pearls

Marking special events like birthdays, graduations, or weddings, pearls are one of the most popular pieces found in many jewelry boxes. Inside my sister-in-law's jewelry box, which I inherited, I found a unique pearl brooch. I'm sorry she is not here to share the history behind it. This intriguing antique looks like it would have quite an interesting story to tell.

Made of gold, onyx, and small diamond chips, the focal piece is a large pearl the size of a small bird's egg. On either side of the large pearl are two small pearl clusters formed in the shape of flowers. The gold work that lassoes around the pearls and other jewels is ornate and full of intricate details.

Looking at the big pearl in the middle of the brooch, reminds me of the pearly gates of heaven mentioned in Revelation. Inspired to find out more, I read *Revelation 21:21* which says, *"And the twelve gates were twelve pearls: each individual gate was of one pearl. And the street of the city was pure gold like transparent glass."* All I can say is, "Wow! How awesome is that?"

I have lots of questions about the pearly gates which have inspired over 334 secular songs by 14 artists and 72 albums. Additionally, there are numerous hymns. I want to know how tall each gate will be? Will they be round or cut in half? Is there a door knob? If so, what does it look like? Regardless, I want to actually see them.

I do believe the gates of pearls are real. They were purchased by Jesus who paid for my redemption and forgave all my sins. Truly, heaven is a destination no one should miss.

Our minds are too finite to even comprehend the place God has prepared for those who believe. If you need more information about how you can be assured of seeing the pearly gates, please look at the back of our book for more information.

☦ Carolyn

Jewelry Gems

"Jesus said unto him, "'I am the way, the truth, and the life. No one comes to the Father except through Me."'
John 14:6

1. Look inside your jewelry box and see if you can find a piece that reminds you of heaven. Record your findings and explain the connection. Share your thoughts with someone close to you. _____

_____

_____

_____

2. Read *Revelation 21:15-21* and record your thoughts and questions. _____

_____

_____

_____

"But as it is written: "Eye has not seen, nor ear heard, nor have entered into the heart of man, the things which God has prepared for those who love Him."
I Corinthians 2:9

Pearls and the Purple Pendant

"Blessed be the God and Father of our Lord Jesus Christ, who has blessed us with every spiritual blessing in the heavenly places in Christ, just as He chose us in Him before the foundation of the world, that we should be holy and without blame before Him in love, having predestined us to adoption as sons by Jesus Christ to Himself, according to the good pleasure of His will, to the praise of the glory of His grace, by which He made us accepted in the Beloved."

Ephesians 1:3-6

Every girl needs a good strand of pearls to wear. I have several, some that are good quality and some not so good; but, still fun to have. There is a specific one that I attach to a beautiful purple starburst pendant. I love wearing this necklace because it reminds me of family.

In *Ephesians 1*, there are many promises of spiritual blessings. We are beloved by God. As a believer I am part of God's *family.*

I have an eternal home that is being prepared for me as stated in *John 14:1-4*. This is part of the hope that we have as believers for our future.

✞ Terri

Jewelry Gems

"Let not your heart be troubled; you believe in God, believe also in Me. In My Father's house are many mansions; if it were not so, I would have told you. I go to prepare a place for you. And if I go and prepare a place for you, I will come again and receive you to Myself; that where I am, there you may be also. And where I go you know, and the way you know."
John 14:1-4

Re-write this verse inserting your name. Make it your prayer to God.

Tarnished by Time

"Do not lay up for yourselves treasures on earth, where moth and rust destroy and where thieves break in and steal; but lay up for yourselves treasures in heaven, where neither moth nor rust destroys and where thieves do not break in and steal. For where your treasure is, there your heart will be also."
Matthew 6:19-21

When my children were younger, every summer we vacationed in a condo my parents owned in Red River, New Mexico. Always on the agenda was a trip to the Taos Pueblo. Ancient ruins indicate Native Americans lived there over 1,000 years ago. Pueblo tradition dictates there can be no electricity or running water inside the Pueblo walls. Most members of the tribe occupy more modern homes in town, but also keep their traditional home inside the Pueblo for ceremonies. However, approximately 150 people still live within the walls full-time. It was fun to walk around and travel back in time.

After visiting the ancient Native American compound, we always enjoyed shopping around the Taos town square looking for bargains and treasures. That is where I found my storyteller pin. It was shiny brass with a replica of some of the adobe homes in the Pueblo. Hanging down from the homes were a plethora of shiny charms and beads including a sun, cactus, moon, coyote, raven, and some storytelling people. I loved it because I could take a little bit of the Pueblo home with me to remember the wonderful heritage and culture of Taos.

My mind would go crazy thinking about all the stories I could come up with the trinkets on the pin. When I found it recently, I discovered time had stolen its shine and tarnished it. Gone also are family vacations to Red River, yet my happy vacation memories still remain. The pin is in good shape, but it will take a lot of polishing to get it looking shiny and new again.

I don't imagine I'll be taking the tarnished pin, or any of my jewelry, to heaven when I die. What I will take is all the memories I have of sharing Jesus with others and my hope of heaven.

I believe I'll see many people there because I told them about Jesus. I can hardly wait to live in a place where there is no sickness or pain. A place where water runs freely and streets are made of gold. I get all giddy and excited just thinking about it.

If you want to invest in something that will never tarnish, share the good news with as many people as you can. The 1,000-year-old Pueblo is very impressive, but heaven is eternal. It is one destination you cannot afford to miss.

✞ Carolyn

Jewelry Gems

1. Have you ever invested in something that quickly tarnished or was ruined? How did that make you feel? If you are looking for a good investment, we would like to invite you to invest in G.A.L.S.O. which is God's Amazing Love Story Orphanage located in Zambia, Africa. You can find out more about it at www.GodsAmazingLoveStorytellers.com. E.P.I. information is on pages 202-203. Contact www.evangelismpartners.org.

1. Journal about your best investment. _____

_____
_____
_____
_____
_____
_____

2. Read *John 14:1-3, Isaiah 35:5-6,* and *Philippians 3:21.* Then record your thoughts about heaven. What are you most excited about? _____

_____
_____
_____
_____
_____
_____
_____

Chapter 5

To Help Others Understand New Life in Christ

"Therefore we were buried with Him through baptism into death, that just as Christ was raised from the dead by the glory of the Father, even so we also should walk in newness of life."

Romans 6:4

Pure Heart

There's nothing more precious than receiving a gift from someone who has a pure heart. It is priceless! I was the recipient of such a gift one afternoon. My very young grandson, Caedmon, had purchased this present at his school's Christmas gift store. He could hardly wait to give it to me. Looking into his beautiful, excited blue eyes, I accepted the gift.

My grandson had chosen a pink stone ring nestled in a pink plastic box with a lovely pink bow on top. It was a masterpiece, and I received it with exaggerated joy! Caedmon then told me all the details of his shopping trip. I hugged him and put on the ring. Then we had to decide where to keep the pretty pink box. It could not be hidden away. NO! The ledge above the kitchen sink was where my grandson decided it should be placed so everyone could see it. Then, when I took my ring off to do dishes, or fix dinner, pepperoni pizza preferred, it would be right there for me.

Today, a few years later, the prized jewelry box is still in the prime spot on the ledge. Funny, too, is that I see my grandson occasionally check it out to see if the ring is still inside the box! I love the innocent faith of children, so does Jesus!

♪Linda

Jewelry Gems

"Assuredly, I say to you, whoever does not receive the kingdom of God as a little child will by no means enter it."
Mark 10:15 and Luke 18:17

1. Describe a priceless gem similar to mine that you have either given or received. _____

_____

_____

_____

_____

2. The Father God gave us His priceless gift in Jesus. Write about what this means to you._____

_____

_____

_____

_____

_____

_____

_____

_____

_____

Cross Collection

I have a beautiful collection of jewelry with items in the shape of a cross. When wearing it, I'm reminded of the tremendous sacrifice that Jesus made. Cross jewelry is a great way to share about God's plan! Be ready and equipped to explain its meaning.

A recognizable symbol, the cross represents the Good News of Jesus Christ. Here are the facts: God sent His only Son, Jesus, to come to live on earth, to pay the penalty for our past, present, and future sins and die on the CROSS. Jesus rose on the third day defeating sin and death for eternity!

Let me encourage you! No matter what circumstances and situations you are in, or no matter how sinful you may think you are, the cross is big enough to cover it all.

Jesus only had to die one time to pay the price for ALL sin. If you're a believer and follower of Jesus, when God looks at you, He does not see your sinfulness. God sees you through His Son, Jesus Christ.

✝ Marilyn

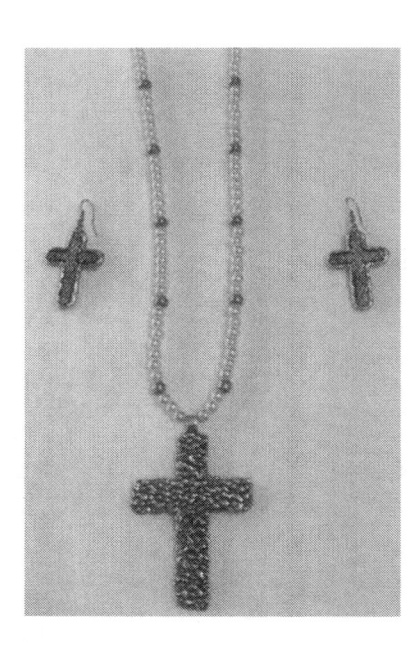

Jewelry Gems

"For God so loved the world that He gave His only begotten Son, that whoever believes in Him should not perish but have everlasting life. For God did not send His Son into the world to condemn the world, but that the world through Him might be saved."
John 3:16-17

1. Describe a piece of jewelry that reminds you of God's everlasting love. _____

_____

_____

_____

_____

_____

_____

2. What does the sacrifice Jesus made on the cross mean to you?

_____

_____

_____

_____

_____

_____

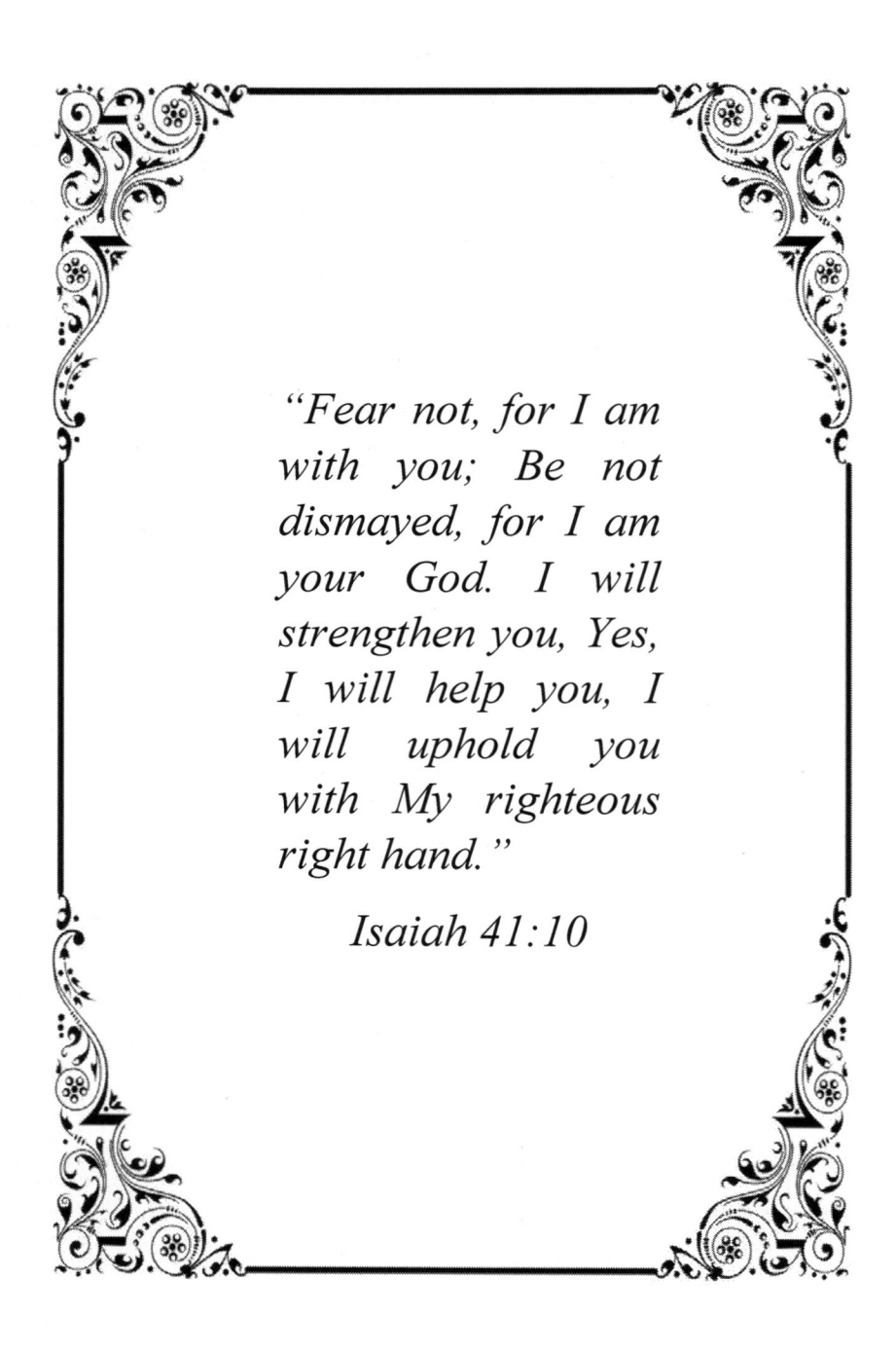

"Fear not, for I am with you; Be not dismayed, for I am your God. I will strengthen you, Yes, I will help you, I will uphold you with My righteous right hand."

Isaiah 41:10

Chapter 6

To See God's Care During Difficult Times

"Be strong and of good courage, do not fear nor be afraid of them; for the LORD your God, He is the One who goes with you. He will not leave you nor forsake you."

Deuteronomy 31:6

Cancer

"You have progressive breast cancer," the specialist informed me. As I rode down the elevator, I felt weak and told my husband I couldn't even walk to the car. Feeling overwhelmed with fear, I cried. My husband guided me to a bench in the hospital where we sat and prayed together.

A verse that I memorized flooded my mind, *"Jesus Christ is the same yesterday, today, and forever." Hebrews 13:8*

Instantly, I felt peace that passes all understanding. I knew that the same **JESUS** who saved me at age seven, was with me at that very moment, and would be with me through the cancer diagnosis, surgery, and treatments.

Later, I had surgery to remove the cancer and received radiation for six weeks. I experienced God's peace throughout the journey. I am nine years CANCER Free!

When I wear my PINK breast cancer earrings, they are constant reminders of my journey. Many comment on my earrings and I share that God will be with them through all life issues … even CANCER!

✝ Marilyn

Jewelry Gems

"And the peace of God, which surpasses all understanding, will guard your hearts and minds through Christ Jesus."
Philippians 4:7

1. Have you, a relative, or friend been diagnosed with cancer or a life threatening illness? How did God minister through the situation? _____

_____

_____

_____

_____

_____

2. How can you share with others so they too can have God's PEACE in hopeless situations? _____

_____

_____

_____

_____

_____

_____

_____

NOTE: The American Cancer Society's estimates for breast cancer in the United States for 2018 states there will be about 266,120 new cases of invasive breast cancer that will be diagnosed in women.

Jewelry's Melody

It has been said that music touches feelings that words cannot. It's the melody of the heart and the voice of the spirit. Maybe that is why I am always drawn to music jewelry. It reminds me to come close to my Savior and share my love and adoration for Him. He is my Friend that *"sticks closer than a brother." Proverbs 18:24*

There are times in life when I find myself at the piano playing and singing songs right out of my spirit. I would like to share the lyrics to one of these songs: *"It Is You"* (copyright 2003).

> *(Chorus) It is You that I run to. It is You I adore*
> *It is You that I count on, You're my refuge in war.*
> *It is You Who runs to meet me. It is You Who understands.*
> *It is You Who holds me closely with Your nail-scarred hands.*
> *(Verse) And You say, "I AM your Banner. On My love you can depend.*
> *I will never ever leave you, I'll stand with you to the end!*
> *For I know the future that the Father has for you.*
> *Because I won this battle long ago, and in Me, you won it, too."*
> *(Verse) On the cross You won the vict'ry, on the cross You overcame*
> *And then hell was split wide open when the Father proclaimed,*
> *"Let Him go! He's not guilty. Satan, you've lost forever more!"*
> *So, Jesus, today I put my own life in Your hands forever more.*
> *Yes, Jesus, today I trust my future in Your hands forever more.*

My precious Jesus helped me through that very difficult time in my life. I will be forever grateful. Have you met my Jesus? If you are not sure, or are searching for meaning in life, I encourage you to read through the lyrics of this song again. Let the Holy Spirit reveal Jesus to you. God loves you more than anyone. He has wonderful plans for your life. It doesn't matter what has been thrown your way. With Jesus, you are never alone. He will guide you to victory.

♪Linda

Jewelry Gems

"For He Himself has said, "I will never leave you nor forsake you." So we may boldly say; "The LORD is my helper; I will not fear. What can man do to me?"
Hebrews 13:5-6

1. When have you given voice to your heart-cry? Describe a piece of jewelry that draws you to the Savior? _____

_____

_____

_____

_____

2. Write how the Lord is your helper. _____

_____

_____

_____

_____

Cystic Fibrosis

A young intern walked in the hospital room and nonchalantly said, "Your daughter has Cystic Fibrosis. It's an incurable and progressive disease. Don't get your hopes up, and don't expect your child to live past the age of thirteen." Afterwards, he quickly walked out of the room.

Stunned, my husband and I held our three-month-old daughter and wept. Overwhelmed with grief and fear, Nolan and I prayed that God would give us strength and wisdom.

The challenge was to live in FEAR or FAITH. We chose to live in FAITH in God and decided to focus on one day at a time. We refused to live in fear or dwell on the fact that Rebekah might die at an early age.

God has been faithful! Through the years, Rebekah has accomplished more than my heart dared to dream. She was a high school cheerleader, received a national award, graduated from high school and college. Now, she is a teacher with five published books. When I wear my treasured Cystic Fibrosis Awareness jewelry, people ask questions. It gives me the opportunity to share about our GREAT and MIGHTY God!

✞ Marilyn

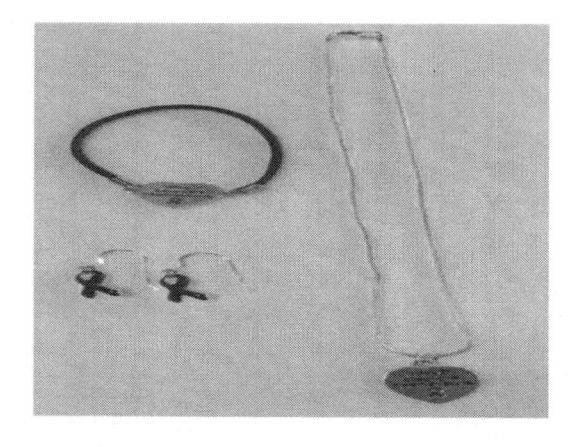

Jewelry Gems

"Call to Me, and I will answer you, and show you great and mighty things, which you do not know."
Jeremiah 33:3

1. Read *Jeremiah 33*. What does it mean to you?_____

_____

_____

_____

2. How can God's Word help you have courage? _____

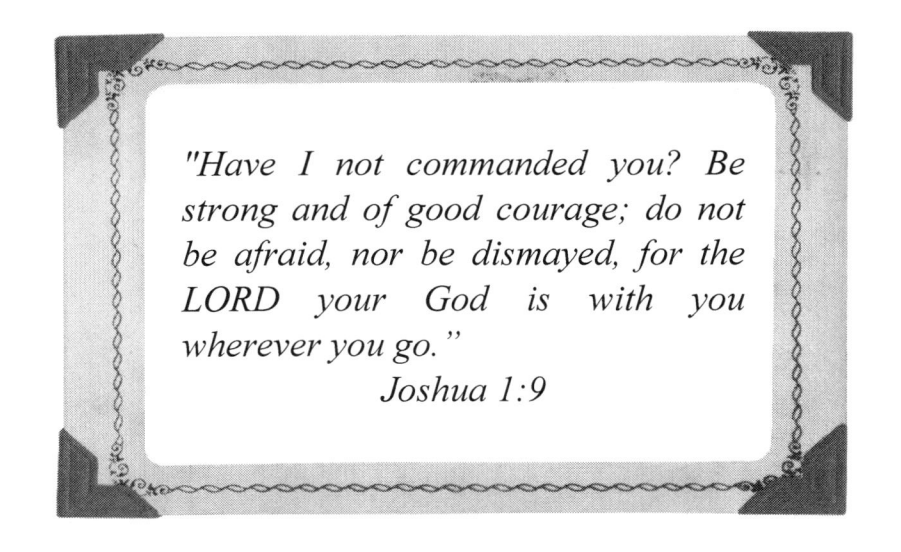

_____

_____

_____

> "Have I not commanded you? Be strong and of good courage; do not be afraid, nor be dismayed, for the LORD your God is with you wherever you go."
> *Joshua 1:9*

Worry Doll

On a vacation to Honduras, I found a worry doll necklace. It consisted of four small handcrafted female dolls. Dressed in traditional Mayan costumes, scraps of traditional woven fabrics were wrapped around the dolls' bodies and heads. Pieces of wood had been twisted together to create their frames, torsos, legs, arms, and heads. Two of the dolls had children in their arms, or by their feet. Others held a broom and a tiny woven basket.

Being a teacher, I asked if there was a story behind the unique necklace. According to a Mayan legend, these dolls are used as a remedy for worrying. Supposedly, when worry keeps a person awake, the worrier tells each doll their problems. Then, they place the dolls under his or her pillow. The dolls take the person's issues so they can sleep peacefully through the night. When morning breaks, the person wakes up refreshed.

It's a cute story, and I loved the necklace enough to buy it. I have a much better solution to getting a good night's sleep. *Exodus 33:14* has a promise from God. It says, *"My Presence will go with you, and I will give you rest."*

When we focus our attention on the Lord, we can be sure He can handle every situation. Worry is actually doubting that God cares for us and can handle our problems. Whenever we find ourselves worrying, repent and turn to God. Claim that His presence will never leave.

✝ Carolyn

Jewelry Gems

"You will keep him in perfect peace, whose mind is stayed on You, because he trusts in You."
                              Isaiah 26:3

List your problems. After you have done this, write the following statement in big capital letters under them. I do not need to tell my problems to God. I need to tell my problems that I serve a big capable God.

1. Write down examples of God's faithfulness to you in the past and focus on God, not your worries. _____

_____

_____

_____

2. Read *Luke 12:24-30.* Write in your own words what the passage means to you. _____

_____

_____

Butterfly Promise

As a second grade teacher, I ordered caterpillars each year for a science experience. Students could observe the stages of the butterfly. The experience of watching the transformation was a great way to reinforce faith with children as they observed the miraculous change.

The butterfly metamorphosis transformed a tiny egg to an ugly and fuzzy caterpillar then to a hidden chrysalis. Finally, it became a breathtaking butterfly. This process is an amazing resurrection symbol. Jesus Christ was born, crucified, buried in a tomb, and rose as the victorious Savior.

I received this butterfly necklace and earrings as a gift from my children for Mother's Day. When people comment on my jewelry, it gives me the opportunity to share the Christian symbolism.

Butterfly jewelry is a reminder of the caterpillar's struggle to become a new creation. It assures me that God is the awesome creator and masterful artist. When I wear my butterfly jewelry, I'm reminded of God's promises in the Bible. I want to share this Good News with others!

✟ Marilyn

Jewelry Gems

"Therefore, if anyone is in Christ, he is a new creature; old things have passed away; behold, all things have become new."
II Corinthians 5:17

1. What does the symbolism of the metamorphosis of a caterpillar to a butterfly mean to you? _____

_____

_____

_____

_____

2. What does it mean to become a new creature in Christ as referenced in *II Corinthians 5:17*? _____

_____

_____

_____

_____

_____

_____

Pure Love

The cross of Jesus is lovely to wear, however, that scene in His life was anything but pretty. When I wear the jewelry, it brings double emotions of humility and ecstatic joy. Does that sound mixed-up to you? Let me explain.

An internationally respected minister once shared an experience he had with the Lord that forever changed the relationship I have with my Savior. The featured speaker stood backstage and told the Lord he was not going to go out there in front of all those people. When asked why, he reminded Jesus about the specific sin committed that day. The Lord said He didn't know what he was talking about. Then the minister reminded Him about his repenting and asking for forgiveness that very afternoon. Jesus inquired if the minister believed the Word of God. Puzzled, the minister replied, "Of course!" In *Isaiah 43:25,* it is recorded that Jesus forgives and forgets our sins when we repent before Him. Then the Lord told him, *"Son, don't run from Me when you sin, run to Me."*

God knows us best and has made provision for us to walk in fellowship with Him every day, no matter what happens. It is so true what Jesus said to the disciples, *"The spirit indeed is willing, but the flesh is weak." Mark 14:38*

When I look at the special earrings, I am humbled knowing that *my sins* put Jesus on the cross. He is not there now, though, He is risen and sitting at the right hand of God, the Father Almighty! Forever changed, I am dancing in ecstatic joy realizing that my sins are forgiven and forgotten by Jesus.

My desire is to live my life in such a way that brings joy to my Savior. When I "mess up," *I RUN to Him*, rather than hide. It is never a good idea to be out of fellowship with the Lord. He paid the ultimate price because of His pure love for each of us. It is my hope and prayer that your life be touched by this minister's experience.

♪Linda

Jewelry Gems

"My little children, these things I write to you, so that you may not sin. And if anyone sins, we have an Advocate with the Father, Jesus Christ the righteous. And He Himself is the propitiation for our sins, and not for ours only but also for the whole world."
I John 2:1-2

1. Write your reaction to the minister's experience with the Lord.

_____

_____

_____

_____

2. What jewelry do you have that draws your attention to the Lord's sacrifice and provision? Share what Jesus has revealed to you after a "mess up." _____

_____

_____

_____

_____

Perfect Plan

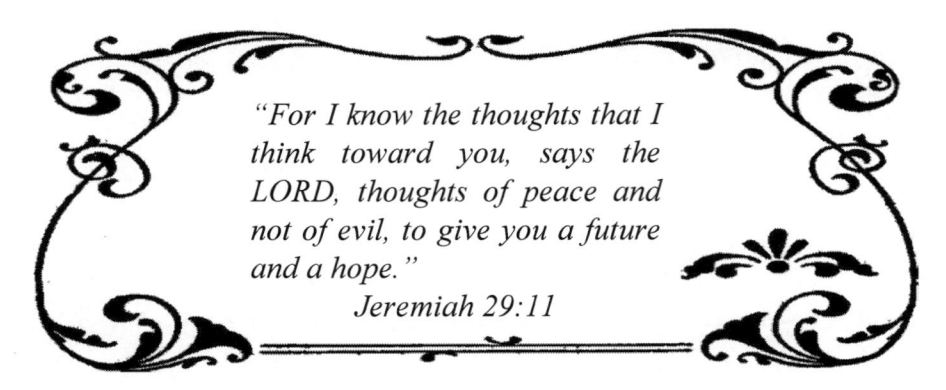

> *"For I know the thoughts that I think toward you, says the LORD, thoughts of peace and not of evil, to give you a future and a hope."*
> *Jeremiah 29:11*

Making plans and having things organized in my mind and on paper fills me with peace. I hate it when I have difficult situations and there are no answers in sight.

Recently, it could have been easy for me to get overwhelmed like I've done in the past. This time, I was determined to give my problems to God and let Him solve them. I told God, *I don't have a plan. I need your plan for me.*

Picking up a book by Kay Arthur, I began reading. On every page, she talked about *Jeremiah 29:11 NIV, "For I know the plans I have for you, declares the Lord; plans to prosper you and not to harm you, plans to give you a hope and a future."* When I had my quiet time, my Bible fell open to *Jeremiah 29:11*. I went to a Christian bookstore, and right in the entrance, was a print of the same verse. The Lord was telling me not to worry because He had a plan; not just any random plan, but a really good one, so I could relax and trust Him.

The icing on the cake was my birthday present from my son, Cole, and his wife, Christy. It was a very unique necklace written in Morse code. You guessed it. The special necklace said *Jeremiah 29:11*. Once again, it was God's way of assuring me that I didn't need to take matters in my hands. God had everything worked out in His perfect plan.

✝ Carolyn

Jewelry Gems

1. Record ways you can distinguish if your thoughts are your own or from God. _____

_____

_____

_____

_____

2. Describe a time when your plan wasn't nearly as good as God's.

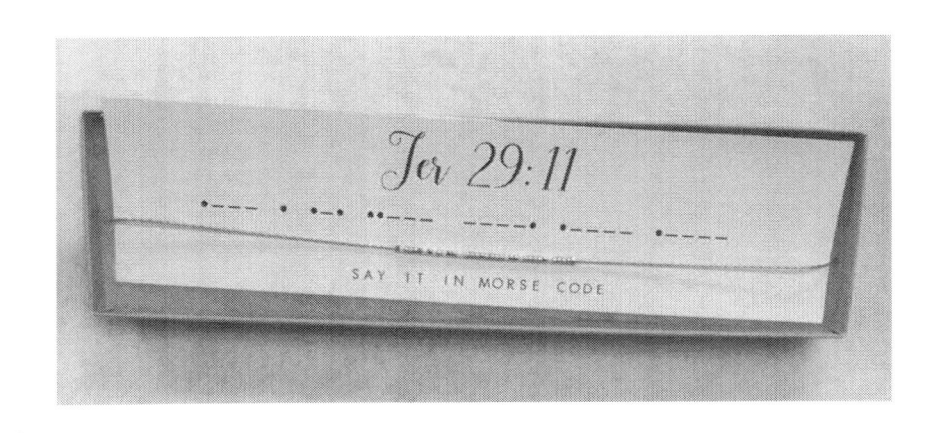

_____

_____

_____

_____

_____

Always There

When I thought God wasn't listening
He heard my every prayer
When I felt the loneliest
He stood close beside me, always there

When I couldn't see Him working
He was creating His perfect plan
Even in the darkest times
My name was inscribed upon His hand

No tear of mine has gone unnoticed
No petition has been unheard
So I'll stand firm on His promises

And trust in the faithfulness of His Word!

✞ Carolyn

Noises of Life

I have a pair of purple dangly earrings made of seashells individually hooked together. When I wear them, they touch the top of my shoulder. Sometimes, the noise from my earrings is just too much to handle, so I have to take them off. That is like our life. We get so busy and involved that we can't stop. We forget the purpose we were made. We can't focus on the reason for our life because the noise of life gets in the way. This is exactly what Satan desires. He wants to distract us from everything thinking he has won.

My pastor said in a sermon recently, we sometimes look so hard and long at our problems that we only glance in the direction of Christ. This must change. We need to transfix our focus on Christ. Problems need to be something that we simply glance at. When focused on Christ, we can do the impossible! Did you know that Christ resides in the impossible? *He makes impossible possible!*

A great example is in *Matthew 14:22-33*. Jesus had His disciples get into a boat and they went to the other side. Jesus went by Himself to pray. Later, the boat was in the middle of the sea. It was tossed about by the waves. The wind was fierce. The disciples were disturbed when they saw Jesus. The group thought they were seeing a ghost.

Read *Matthew 14:27-31*, *"But immediately Jesus spoke to them, saying, "Be of good cheer! It is I; do not be afraid." And Peter answered Him and said, "Lord, if it is You, command me to come to You on the water." So He said, "Come." And when Peter had come down out of the boat, he walked on the water to go to Jesus. But when he saw that the wind was boisterous, he was afraid; and beginning to sink he cried out, saying, "Lord, save me!" And immediately Jesus stretched out His hand and caught him."*

Christ was a life saver that day. He grabbed Peter's hand and lifted him out of the water. Remember that He is the ruler of everything, creator of all things. He resides in the impossible!

When the noises of life get you distracted and take you into a place that is dark and deep, raise your hands! Cry out to God. He promises that you won't be alone!

✝ Terri

Jewelry Gems

"I will never leave you nor forsake you."
Hebrews 13:5b

All you have to do is reach out your hand and say His name, Jesus! He will grab you by the hand and lift you up! He will make your impossible, possible and allow you to walk on the water of life.

What distractions are keeping you from Christ?_____

_____
_____
_____
_____
_____
_____
_____
_____
_____
_____
_____

Raise your hands and pray. Ask Jesus to help you get out of the muck and mire of life to make your **impossible, possible**!

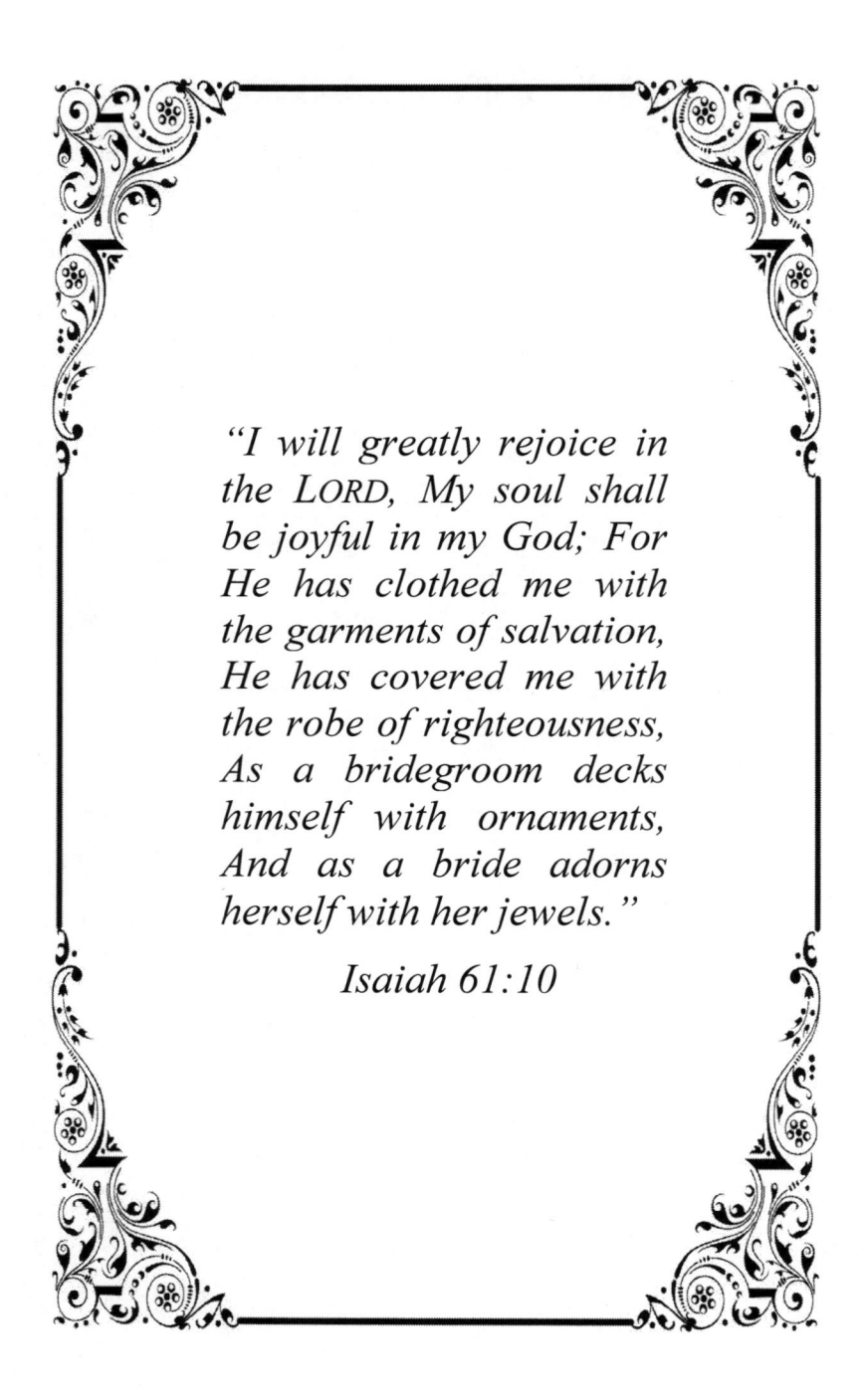

"I will greatly rejoice in the LORD, My soul shall be joyful in my God; For He has clothed me with the garments of salvation, He has covered me with the robe of righteousness, As a bridegroom decks himself with ornaments, And as a bride adorns herself with her jewels."

Isaiah 61:10

Chapter 7

To Remember Covenant Relationships

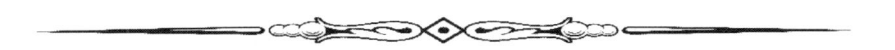

"Therefore what God has joined together, let not man separate."

Mark 10:9

Wedding Band

In 1972, Nolan and I had our wedding bands created in gold by our friend, Ed Covington. The unique design represents the four seasons. Little did we know that this would be symbolic of our marriage. The design begins as a bare branch, and emerges as a bud, and ends in full bloom.

Through the seasons of our marriage, we have grown spiritually. During the "Spring," we sought God's will for our marriage and studied the Bible together for guidance. The "Summer" was when we put on the armor of God to equip us for life's daily battles. "Autumn" brought hardships and trials with a child who was born with an incurable and progressive disease.

There were frequent hospitalizations and sicknesses which were difficult, but we witnessed miracles of God's healing hands time and time again. We are now in the "Winter" of marriage. Our theory of stronger together has proven true year after year! We praise our mighty God for the power to conquer daily battles. Stress, fear, financial obligations, and even dealing with an incurable disease only increases our faith in God.

Our marriage is stronger now than when we first made the wedding vows in 1972. The reason is … we love each other, pray constantly together, communicate daily, and have faith in God. Our wedding band is a constant reminder of the seasons of marriage and how God is always present.

✟ Marilyn

Jewelry Gems

"To everything there is a season, A time for every purpose under heaven."
                              Ecclesiastes 3:1

1. Describe your wedding band or favorite piece of jewelry and the reason it was chosen. _____
_____
_____
_____

2. How has God strengthened you through the seasons of your life?
_____
_____
_____
_____

The Silver Tie

"The LORD their God will save them in that day, As the flock of His people. For they shall be like the jewels of a crown, Lifted like a banner over His land."
Zechariah 9:16

I remember my mom really likes turquoise jewelry and a specific piece was what I called "the silver tie." This necklace got the name because it wasn't like all her other pieces, it was different. Instead of a clasp it went straight over mom's head and once in place you could move the turquoise starburst up or down depending on where you wanted it to be placed. Then on both ends of the chain were turquoise bobbles; I liked them to be uneven, I thought it made it even fancier!

When I became a teenager, I was less impressed with "the silver tie" and more engaged with other things. Occasionally, I would talk jewelry with my mom, but really I was all about my friends and such. This is the normal progression of life, right?

I'll never forget the day when my mom walked into church with her necklace on. *Beautiful* I thought. She sat down and proceeded to do whatever she was doing when my oldest child walked up to my mom and plopped down on her lap. My daughter couldn't spit out the "gr" so called her "Anma" and began to play with "the silver tie" necklace.

Floods of memories rushed to my mind. I began to tear up. I thought *maybe my daughter would have her own "silver tie" memory.*

Little did I know, that day my mom was sharing something much greater than a necklace with her granddaughter. My precious mom was sharing Jesus!

✟ Terri

Jewelry Gems

1. Who can you share Jesus with today? _____
_____
_____
_____

2. Who in your family needs to have an open heart to God? Write a prayer for each one. _____
_____
_____
_____
_____
_____
_____
_____
_____

My Beloved

"I am my beloved's, and my beloved is mine."
Song of Solomon 6:3

About five years ago, my husband, Joe, and I had the privilege of going to the Holy Land. We were there on our 42nd wedding anniversary. I don't see how that anniversary can ever be topped.

As a couple, we went to the Garden of Gethsemane and prayed; then we toured other sites and shopped. That night, our tour guide took us to meet a jeweler. Joe hit the jackpot. He got me a new wedding band written in Hebrew that said, "I am my beloved's and my beloved is mine."

I cherish that ring and the sentiment it represents every day. With each day and year, I love my husband more and thank God for him.

Marriage is not easy but worth it. I'm so grateful to have a lifetime partner to go through the different seasons of life, both good and bad.

What makes a marriage strong is having Christ at the center. Being in a covenant relationship with God has made us one. Even though Joe and I have been married a long time, we are still learning about each other and believe the best is yet to be as we grow old together.

We took a marriage enrichment class at our church. I imagine people thought *What are you two doing in here?* Our marriage is strong, but we want to make it even stronger with each passing year.

Both of us thoroughly enjoyed the class. We learned how to love each other according to *I Corinthians 13*. Commitment, grace, and forgiveness are key things we continue to work on. *"I am for my beloved and my beloved is mine."* He is God's gift to me.

♡ Carolyn

Jewelry Gems

1. What do you think are some of the most important things that go into making a strong marriage or relationship? Explain your answer.

2. How do you maintain Christ-centered relationships during difficult times?

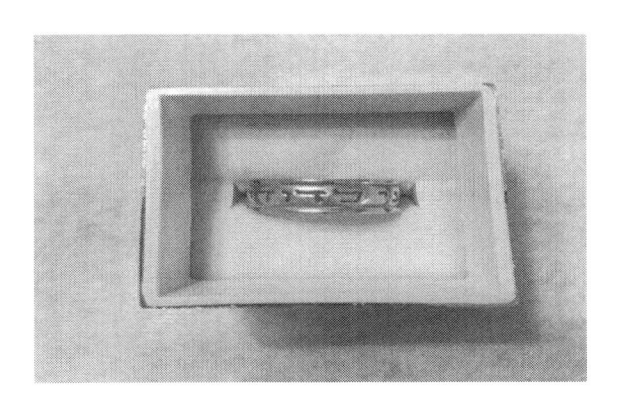

"A good man leaves an inheritance to his children's children."

Proverbs 13:22

Chapter 8

To Pass Along a Godly Legacy

"You shall love the Lord your God with all your heart, with all your soul, and with all your strength. And these words which I command you today shall be in your heart. You shall teach them diligently to your children, and shall talk of them when you sit in your house, when you walk by the way, when you lie down, and when you rise up."

Deuteronomy 6:5-7

Roots

"For he shall be like a tree planted by the waters, Which spreads out its roots by the river."
Jeremiah 17:8a

I inherited a tree pendant from my mom. It is very ornate and gorgeous. The only concern would be wearing it. When would I? Where would I? Wearing it on a cardigan sweater didn't look very good. A jacket; I'm not really the jacket person anymore! I closed my eyes and thought, what occasion did my mom wear it? Ah-ha, she wore it on a fancy black pullover with a solid scarf.

Next thing I knew, I found myself heading to the recesses of my closet looking for the perfect scarf - hmm, just the right one ... beautiful royal purple. Stunning! Just looking at the pendant on my scarf, around my neck, brought back a flood of memories.

Suddenly, I was a young girl again and could almost smell mom's perfume surrounding me. There I was, wanting to return to that special time. It is in these moments filled with recollections of the past when I have the opportunity to share with my kids these same kind of experiences to build their memories.

These are the "roots" that grow down deep connecting us one with others in our families. Christ wants these same connections with His children. Roots grow deep to the water of life which fills us up and builds our faith. ***Roots ... trees ... families!***

God includes all believers in His family. We need to share our connection to Him with others, so they have the opportunity to become participants in the inheritance as well. Each of us has a "roots" story. Don't be hesitant to share it with your family, friends, and even strangers. You never know what effect your story will have on them.

✝ Terri

Jewelry Gems

1. Name something you inherited, both from family and from God._____

_____

_____

_____

2. Write a memory about the item. _____

_____

_____

_____

3. Name something you would like to pass along to your family.

_____

_____

_____

_____

Daddy's Ring

As far back as I can remember, this is the only ring I ever saw my daddy wear. In the earliest days of my life, he worked in the oil fields. Daddy did not wear the ring for safety reasons. Later, when he worked as a computer programmer, the ring made an appearance on a finger.

With a diamond in the middle of two rubies, it was set in a masculine gold band. Thrilled and blessed, I inherited this treasure. The ring held special significance for my dad. I can't say for sure, but it may have been his wedding ring.

Daddy wasn't one to wear jewelry. On very special occasions, however, you would see him with cuff links and a bolo tie. He and my mother loved to dance and were members of a square dance club at one time. Mother influenced him to wear beautiful matching outfits … his shirt and her dress of the same material. They were a stunning couple.

When I look at the three stones in his ring, it reminds me of how my daddy was powerful, loving, and dependable to me and our family. He was a good man to all. Even so, my daddy rose to a higher level of honor in my eyes when he gave his heart to Jesus and was baptized with the family when I was 14 years old. The stones took on new meaning: the diamond is the Father God, the rubies are Jesus, the Son, and the Holy Spirit.

My daddy, at age 83, went to his Father's house. I am so very confident that he heard God say, *"Well done, good and faithful servant." Matthew 25:21*

We are instructed in the Word to live our lives in honor and glory to God. I can think of no better way than loving others and sharing the gospel.

Each of us has been given gifts and treasures that are unique to use in our special assignments. Be faithful with those and aspire to hear praise from your heavenly Father.

♪ Linda

Jewelry Gems

"Well done, good and faithful servant."
Matthew 25:21a

1. What heirloom jewelry do you own? Write the story. _____

_____

_____

_____

_____

2. How can you use those memories to draw others to our Lord?

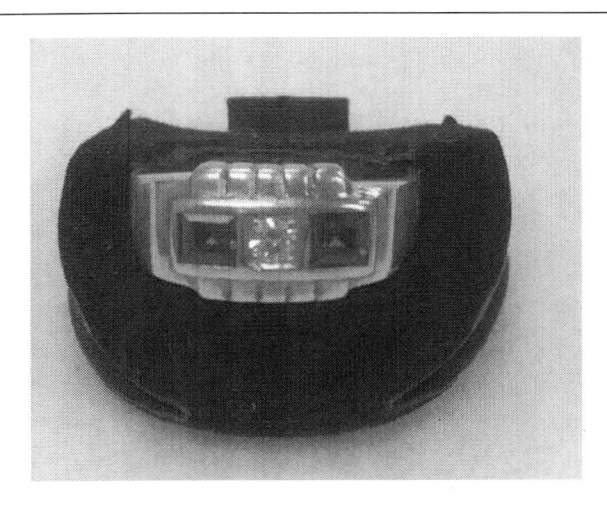

_____

_____

_____

_____

A Good Name

My husband, Joe, and I met in college on a blind date. His roommate was dating my roommate. They thought it would be hilarious to set us up. We were so opposite they thought we would hate each other. I guess the laugh was on them because they broke up, and we married two years later.

At the University of Arkansas, girls living in my dorm had to sign out before they left. Dormitory students had to write the time we left, who we were with, where we were going, and what time we planned to be back. For about a month or two I wrote that I was going out with Joe Hitchcock. One day, Joe was watching me sign out and he said, "Who's Joe Hitchcock?"

"You, Silly," I replied.

"No, I'm not. Don't you even know my name?"

Perplexed, I said, "For two months, I have thought that's your name."

"Well, for two months you've been wrong. My name is Joe Hedgecock, not Joe Hitchcock," he informed me.

"Ok then," I said, surprised that it took me so long to know my future husband's real name. He told me his name originated in Ireland. The English didn't want the Irish to learn to read or write. His clan hid behind hedges when having lessons. There had to be a lookout, so they wouldn't get caught. If the lookout saw someone coming, he would begin crowing like a rooster.

Apparently, Joe's family took turns being the lookout and thus got the name "Hedgecock." It's cool because our family has valued learning.

My precious daughter-in-law, Christy, gave me a bronze bracelet with "Hedgecock" engraved on it. My prayer is that each of my children and grandchildren spend their lives building good names for themselves that will make God and our families proud.

✞ Carolyn

Jewelry Gems

"A good name is to be chosen rather than great riches, loving favor rather than silver and gold."
Proverbs 22:1

1. Why do you think the Bible says that a good name is better than great riches? _____

_____

_____

_____

2. What is the meaning and origin or your name? _____

_____

_____

3. How does a person build a good reputation? Read *Proverbs 19:23 a*nd locate other verses in Proverbs that are clues to building a good name. _____

_____

_____

Floral Brooch

"And I have declared to them Your name, and will declare it, that the love with which You loved Me may be in them, and I in them."
John 17:26

As far back as I can remember, the floral brooch and earbobs accented many of mother's wardrobe choices. They were usually the set most often selected for a more formal affair. I don't know where they came from. I suspect they were a gift from a church member. I do know the set must be at least fifty years old and possibly older.

Really, I never considered the brooch and earbobs of any worth until my mother passed away twenty plus years ago. I found them in her jewelry box days after her funeral. I recalled the many times they adorned her outfits. Suddenly, they became worthy of my attention and care.

The set is now a cherished possession. Not because of their monetary value, but because of who owned them. For a reason I do not know, my mother demonstrated significant regard for the pieces. She held on to them and wore them for over fifty years.

Curious how that works: she loved the set and wore them frequently. Upon her death the brooch and earbobs suddenly became important to me. They took on new meaning and became significant simply because the set belonged to my mother.

In a more profoundly significant way, Jesus cherished His Father's name. He spoke it often, always with great admiration and love. Jesus relished in His Father's love and wanted His followers to experience that same loving approval. He knew that if His followers loved Him they would love His Father as well. The Father was in Him, and He was in the Father. What He cherished, they too would cherish.

✝ Sharon

Jewelry Gems

As we grow older, sometimes memories of the past help us recall the importance of the present. A simple pin set of Mom's has caused me to ponder and reflect on her life. Although the set was cared for, it did not define who she was. Perhaps the marked pages of Mom's Bible better define her than any other item.

1. What item in your jewelry box holds a special meaning for you and why? Write out its history; then share it with your family.

_____
_____
_____
_____

2. Identify and write out verses from the Bible that have been the foundation on which you have built your life. Record the significant verses. Pass them on to your family in various forms: recordings, bookmarks, written notes, etc._____

_____
_____
_____

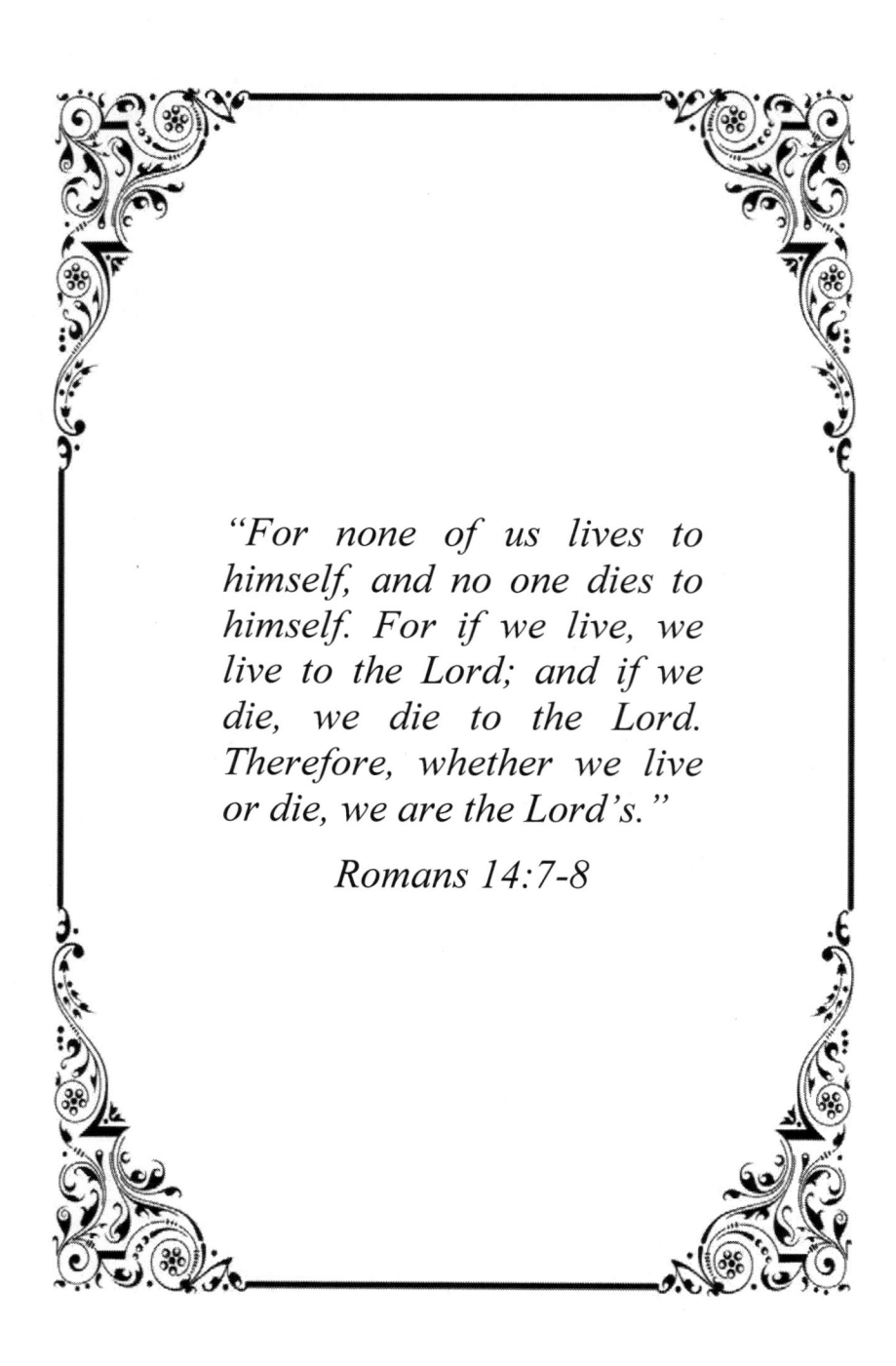

"For none of us lives to himself, and no one dies to himself. For if we live, we live to the Lord; and if we die, we die to the Lord. Therefore, whether we live or die, we are the Lord's."

Romans 14:7-8

Chapter 9

To Know My Identity in Christ

"But as many as received Him, to them He gave the right to become children of God, to those who believe in His name."

John 1:12

The Purple Cord

"And she bound the scarlet cord in the window."
Joshua 2:21

God used Rahab in a mighty way in this Bible story even though she was a "harlot," a woman of questionable character.

First, Rahab hid the men who were spying on the city of Jericho from the king and soldiers. Then, she bravely showed them how to escape by letting the scarlet cord down through her window.

This courageous woman didn't know if she could trust the spies to spare her or her family from destruction. Rahab helped anyway when their army came to take over Jericho.

On the spies' return, the order was given to destroy everything with the exception of Rahab, and her family, who were inside her home. The spies knew the home was Rahab's by the scarlet cord, which was attached to her window!

I was amazed at this story because Rahab became a prominent fixture in the lineage of Christ. If she can be used by God for great things, so can we! I was reminded of this story when I pulled out a purple corded necklace my dad gave me. At the end of the cord before the tassel is a beautiful butterfly encrusted pendant.

I, too, am chosen by God to do great things. While that won't include the lineage of Christ who came to save the world, it does include sharing Him with others who are in desperate need for a Savior!

✝ Terri

Jewelry Gems

1. Who do you know that needs a life line passed to them?

_____

_____

_____

_____

_____

_____

_____

_____

2. Write a prayer for God to give you the right opportunities to share a lifeline with others. _____

_____

_____

_____

_____

_____

_____

_____

_____

_____

Your Name

When we were expecting our daughter, my husband and I spent much thought, prayer, and time selecting her name. We prayerfully chose the Biblical name, Rebekah, which means "captivating" in Hebrew. Her first name is Mary with the Hebrew meaning "child wished for" and has been a family name for five generations. In fact, my mom's first name is Mary.

Many misspelled my daughter's name with "c" instead of "k." So, my sister had two necklaces designed for my daughter with her name, Rebekah. They were her favorites! The necklaces were a reminder of the correct spelling of Rebekah's name.

God placed tremendous significance on names and their meanings. He began with Adam which means, "one formed of the earth." Throughout history, names have been of great importance. When you have Christ in your heart, you belong to Him. God knows who you are, and He knows you by name.

✝ Marilyn

Jewelry Gems

1. What is the meaning of your name? _____

   _____

2. Write *Proverbs 22:1.* _____

   _____

   _____

   _____

3. What does it mean to you that God knows you by name? _____

   _____

   _____

   _____

   _____

> *"Fear not, for I have redeemed you; I have called you by your name; You are Mine."*
>
> *Isaiah 43:1*

Rings of Deception

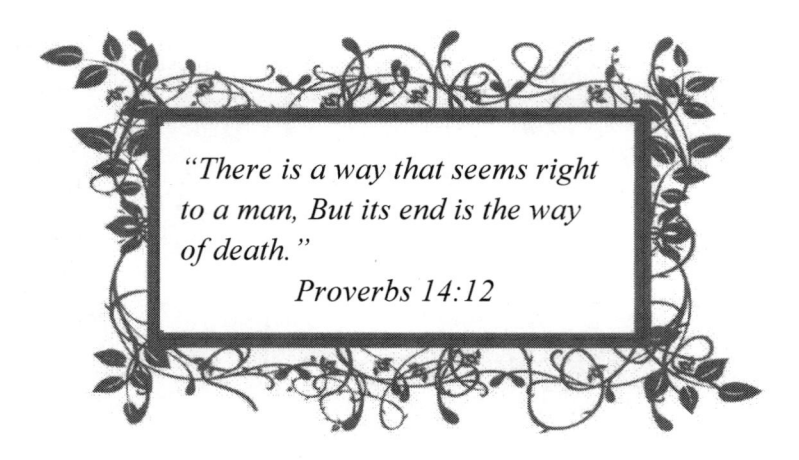

> *"There is a way that seems right to a man, But its end is the way of death."*
> Proverbs 14:12

Thrilled doesn't even begin to describe the emotions which enveloped my heart. Wearing my engagement ring, I was constantly checking the sparkle and dazzle of the stone. It was very small, so I had to hold my hand just right to catch and refract the light into a million glittering prisms. Since we were both in college, funds were short. The stone's size didn't matter at the time; I had a ring, was getting married, and planned to live happily ever after.

Just days after we married, I discovered that my wedding rings were a mismatched set. Bummer! Fast forward ten years. I was still wearing the same mismatched set. Double bummer! I was getting antsy for something a little flashier. After all, I was worth it. So, I did what any self-respecting woman would do, I went out and bought myself a fake ring with a very large stone. I wore that ring proudly until it began to turn colors on my fingers. Then, I bought another and another, keeping up the rhythm for several years. Although each ring I bought had a significant size stone and satisfied a longing, it was still a fake.

Eventually, the silver would wear off revealing their true worth. No longer of value, the rings were thrown, one after another, to the back of a drawer. Why I kept them is a mystery.

I was deceived for years by believing that much of my value was wrapped up in the trappings of this life. I had a wrong belief. I needed the approval of man to measure up. That wrong belief led me into a pattern of deceiving others.

Every ring purchased was another rue in my game of make-believe. People would often comment on the ring I was wearing, I would simply smile and say, "Thank you." Deeply involved in Bible study, God began to pull back the layers of deception and pride. He revealed that the problem wasn't the jewelry I chose to wear, but the attitude of my heart.

✝ Sharon

Jewelry Gems

1. Is there anything in your reality that is deceptive? _____

_____
_____
_____
_____
_____
_____
_____

2. List areas where you have deceived yourself and others. What steps will you take to correct the lies? _____

_____
_____
_____
_____
_____
_____
_____
_____

Chapter 10

To Teach About Stewardship

"For where your treasure is, there your heart will be also."

Matthew 6:21

Simple Pin

*"Train up a child in the way he should go,
And when he is old he will not depart from it."*
Proverbs 22:6

Several days ago, I opened my jewelry catalog and found a tin with all kinds of pins. None of any real value but all held some memory for me. I guess that is why I still have them all.

The one pin that caught my attention I received as a child during the late 50's. I guess pins were the thing. I am not sure why or how this evolved, but a pin was earned in Sunday School for: attendance, Bible brought, offering given, memory verse learned, lesson studied, and for bringing a guest. Apparently, I managed to navigate that successfully because I have the pin to prove it. Now, you may say how ridiculous. But I must tell you, I am grateful for that training.

Thinking back on all the things I learned in that process, I now understand was preparation for my Christian walk. I didn't realize it at the time, but God was equipping me. He was helping me establish a pattern for spiritual growth and maturity.

The practice of being prepared for Sunday has carried over into my adult life. The little pin caused me to stop and recall the benefits of growing up during a time when sound spiritual principles were modeled and taught. Gratefully, this little church pin has served to remind me of the dividends reaped from lessons taught in childhood.

Thank you, Father for drawing back the curtain of time to reveal Your sovereignty in my life. Thank you, for those who taught and equipped me for service. Thank you, that earning a simple pin helped mold and shape my life. Thank you, for constantly reminding me of Your love.

✝ Sharon

Jewelry Gems

1. Write about a lesson you learned as a child that has helped you as an adult. _____

_____

_____

_____

_____

2. Write a prayer to God and thank Him for His Sovereignty. What does that mean to you? _____

_____

_____

_____

_____

My Dad's Necklace

"What does this mean?" I asked my dad when he gave me a necklace with a shovel and a spoon. Not something an eleven-year-old girl would dream about.

"It has a very important message," my dad replied. "Something I hope you will remember all of your life."

Well that's pretty dramatic I thought.

Then my dad began to explain. "The spoon represents what you give God." Everyone knows spoons don't hold much. "Now look at the shovel," Daddy continued. "That's what God gives back to you. Remember you can NEVER out give God!"

That was a valuable lesson my dad taught me at a young age. I have seen the message played out over and over again in my life.

Thank you, Daddy, for the awesome necklace. I love you and appreciate all your wisdom and Godly example.

✝ Carolyn

Jewelry Gems

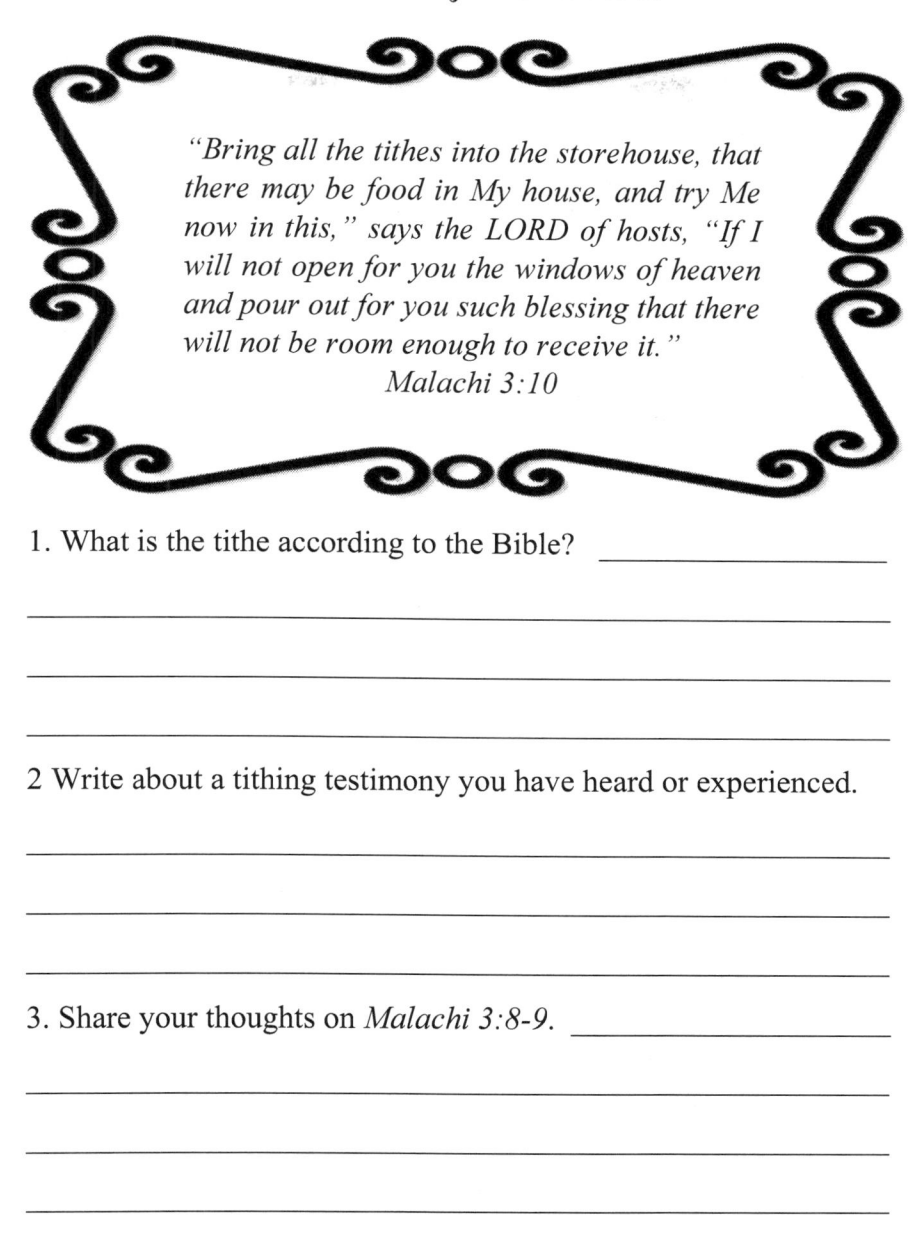

> *"Bring all the tithes into the storehouse, that there may be food in My house, and try Me now in this,"* says the LORD of hosts, *"If I will not open for you the windows of heaven and pour out for you such blessing that there will not be room enough to receive it."*
> Malachi 3:10

1. What is the tithe according to the Bible? _____

_____

_____

_____

2 Write about a tithing testimony you have heard or experienced.

_____

_____

_____

3. Share your thoughts on *Malachi 3:8-9*. _____

_____

_____

_____

A Tangled Mess

A delicate little chain wrapped its tendrils around and through the other pieces of jewelry in the now emptied container. I didn't know how many years that chain had been knotted, but I was determined to untwist the mangled mess. I sat down with tweezers in hand, glasses on, and bright lights glaring.

The tiny elements were almost too closely linked making it difficult for the tweezers to find a good hold. I persisted. An hour later, I had successfully worked one knot free.

Little by little, the chain was released from its bondage. I discovered, much to my dismay, the delicate little chain was broken, thus the reason for it being in a tangled mess in the first place.

Sometimes, our lives become broken. At those times, we may feel we have no value. However, our brokenness is only an opportunity for God to display His magnificent work as the EXPERT jeweler.

God has all the necessary tools needed to untangle the messes of our lives. With tenderness, He restores by gently untangling one knot of pain at a time. He takes His time, and with skillful precision uses the instrument of love to release every difficult entanglement. God polishes us through a process of supernatural refining making us ready for His service.

✞ Sharon

Jewelry Gems

"Ah, Lord GOD! Behold, You have made the heavens and the earth by Your great power and outstretched arm. There is nothing too hard for you."
Jeremiah 32:17

1. Write about a time God has gently untangled a painful event in your life. What were the results of that experience?

_____

_____

_____

_____

_____

2. Tell how God has polished you. For what work has He prepared you? What is preventing you from moving forward?

_____

_____

_____

_____

_____

_____

_____

_____

_____

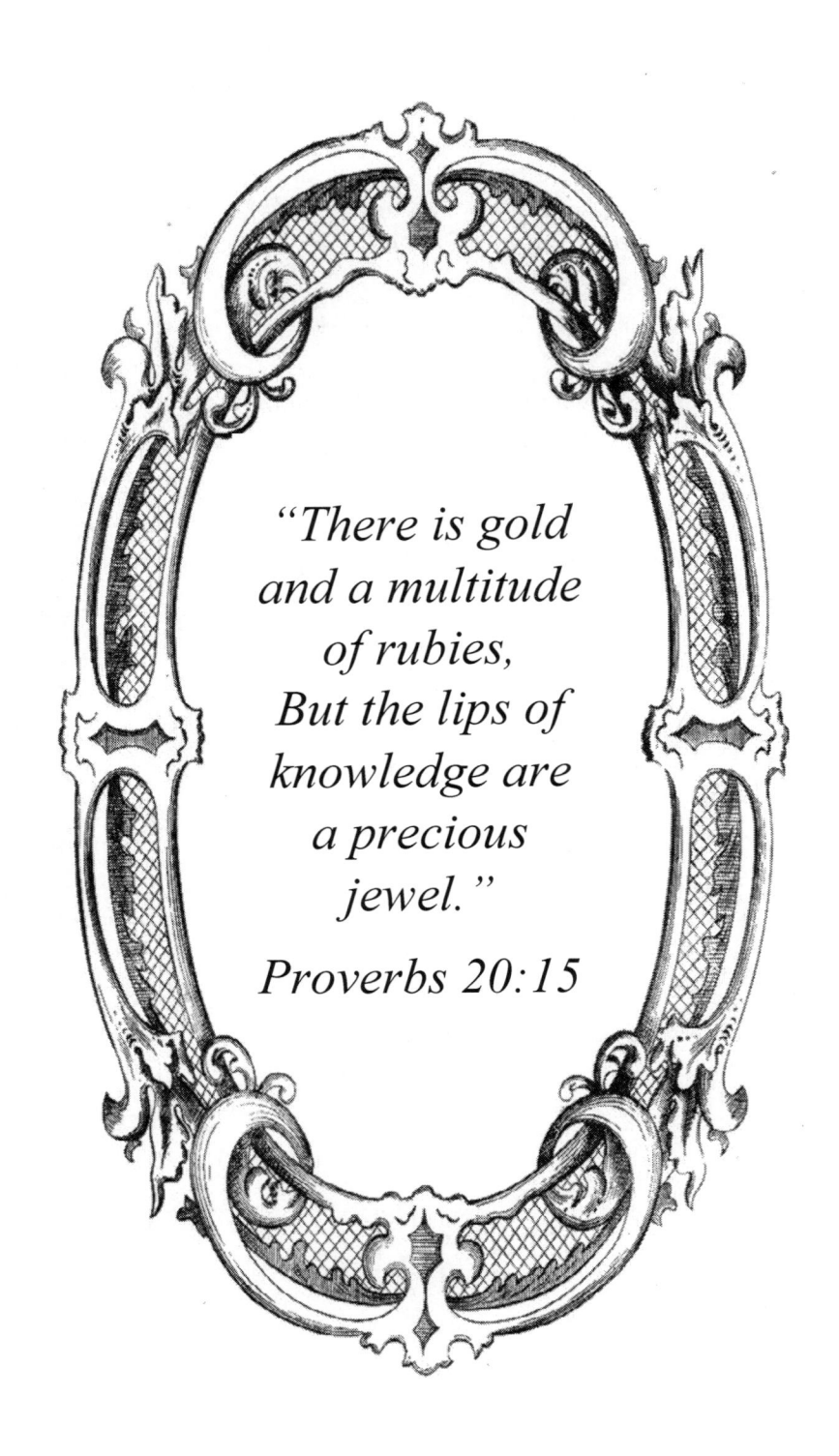

*"There is gold
and a multitude
of rubies,
But the lips of
knowledge are
a precious
jewel."*

Proverbs 20:15

Chapter 11

To Focus on Spiritual Matters and Truths

"The grass withers, the flower fades, But the word of our God stands forever."

Isaiah 40:8

Fruity, Fun Earrings

"But the fruit of the Spirit is love, joy, peace, longsuffering, kindness, goodness, faithfulness, gentleness, self-control. Against such there is no law."
Galatians 5:22-23

I have some fruity, fun earrings that my mom gave me. Every time I wear them I can't help but think of the fruit of the spirit Bible verse. These are attributes that develop as each individual grows in their Christian walk.

LOVE-Christ calls us to love one another in *John 13:34-35*, *"A new commandment I give to you, that you love one another; as I have loved you, that you also love one another. By this all will know that you are My disciples, if you have love for one another."*

JOY-We are to be glad in the Lord and shout for joy as it says in *Psalm 32:11* **"Be glad in the L**ORD **and rejoice, you righteous; And shout for joy, all** you *upright in heart!"*

PEACE-Through Christ, we have immeasurable peace when we rely on Him. *John 14:27*

LONGSUFFERING/PATIENCE-This is hard but attainable when we strive to learn more about Christ. *I Timothy 6:11* states to *"flee these things and pursue ..."* the virtues of God.

KINDNESS-God calls us to have brotherly kindness in verses from *II Peter 1:5-7*, *"...to godliness brotherly kindness ..."*

GOODNESS-*Psalm 16:2* says, *"O my soul, you have said to the LORD, "You are my Lord, My goodness is nothing apart from You."*

FAITHFULNESS-Christ is ever faithful. We are made in His image. We need to reflect His faithfulness as shown in *Psalm 36:5*.

GENTLENESS-Our gentleness as believers should be seen through every aspect of our life because of Christ in us. *II Samuel 22:36*

SELF-CONTROL-This one is difficult but can be achieved through prayer and practice! This is also called restraint. *Proverbs 29:18*

✞ Terri

Jewelry Gems

Write your definitions or references for each attribute.

LOVE
___

JOY
___

PEACE
___

LONGSUFFERING
___

KINDNESS
___

GOODNESS
___

FAITHFULNESS
___

GENTLENESS
___

SELF-CONTROL
___

The Lens

"Looking unto Jesus, the author and finisher of our faith."
Hebrews 12:2a

While rummaging through one of the many drawers of my jewelry box, I discovered a lens from my father's glasses. It lay forgotten for years. The single glass serves as a reminder that God restores sight, both physical and spiritual.

From a very early age, my father's eyesight was compromised. His parents were dirt farmers and barely eked out a living for their family of nine. Eye exams and glasses were luxuries. However, when my grandparents discovered the seriousness of my dad's sight, sacrifices were made to provide for his need … glasses!

When my Dad put them on the first time, his world came into focus. Dad became an insatiable reader. His appetite for learning affected everything he did and who he became. Daddy inspired others to experience the joy of gaining knowledge. God afforded him many roles in life: husband, father, pastor, classroom teacher, coach, and role model. Each character was an opportunity to help others gain proper focus and perspective in life.

Dad's poor sight was a physical condition corrected with the right lens. The appropriate prescription afforded him accurate focus. His life was never the same. Often, our spiritual eye-sight becomes distorted with need for adjustment. The indwelling Holy Spirit provides the necessary correction. God's Word, when applied, pinpoints needed modification. A clarified need for Him evolves, and the wonder of His glory is revealed. The correct spiritual lens changes the trajectory of life.

Dad's eyesight was corrected with the proper lens. Are you having some difficulty focusing on spiritual matters? The Word gives us instruction concerning focus.

✝ Sharon

Jewelry Gems

"For now we see in a mirror, dimly, but then face to face. Now I know in part, but then I shall know just as I also am known."

I Corinthians 13:12

1. What does it mean to have a hunger for learning? Thank God for the beauty of the mind and the ability to learn. Invite the Holy Spirit to adjust your heart to center on Him. _____

_____

_____

_____

_____

2. What is the trajectory of your life? What has become its focus? Ask the Holy Spirit to make the necessary corrections to allow you to see God clearly. _____

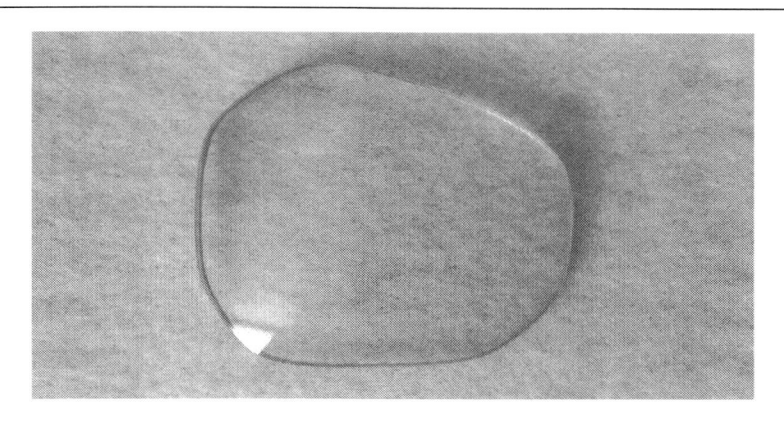

_____

_____

_____

Mother's Pearls

Beautiful pearls have dazzled many an eye. My mother wore pearls in her hair almost every day. She curled her hair each night in order to enjoy the "Shirley Temple" curls during the day. Carefully, my mother pulled the sides and top back into the pearl hair clips leaving wisps of hair to frame her face. She enjoyed many compliments as she went about her day.

Pearls are sparsely mentioned in the Bible. The parable about the pearl of great price is the most referred to Scripture about pearls. In *Matthew 7:6*, Jesus warns us not to cast our pearls to just anyone. He infers that there are those who will reject it, and maybe hurt us.

Have you known anyone who thought they could make another person change their way of thinking? Our Father God has given us free will. Jesus was sent to redeem us from our sins through giving His life in our place. He, alone, is our Savior and Redeemer.

We are not responsible for someone else's decisions. Rather, we are to be wise as serpents and harmless as doves. In other words, we need to follow His advice and flee a potentially harmful situation, not stay and be trampled.

The Word of God is a pearl of great price which can literally save our lives if we heed the wisdom therein. So, as my mother wore the pearls in her hair, it reminds me to keep the Word of God in my mind and praise on my lips. God promises to inhabit my praise.

♪Linda

Jewelry Gems

"Do not give what is holy to the dogs; nor cast your pearls before swine, lest they trample them under their feet, and turn and tear you in pieces."

Matthew 7:6

1. What is God revealing to you in *Matthew 7:6*? _____
_____
_____
_____

2. Write about a time when God gave you wisdom in a difficult situation. _____
_____
_____
_____

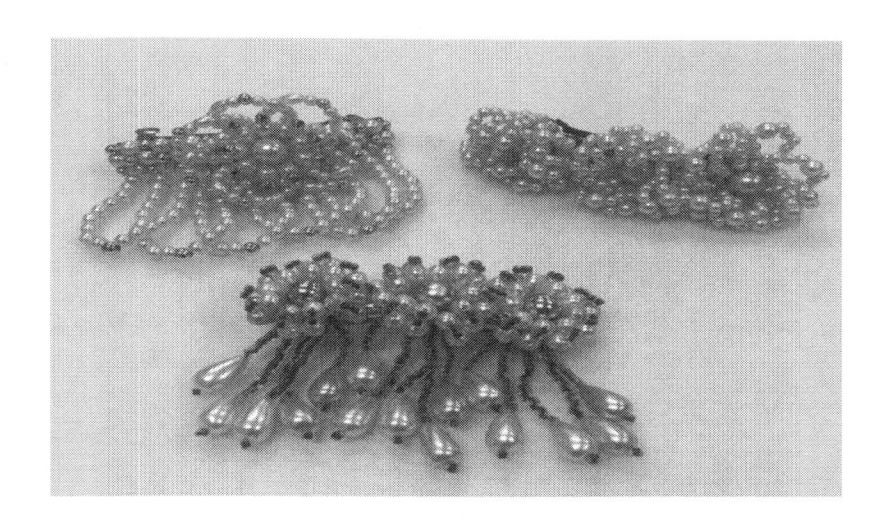

Special Design

"I will praise You, for I am fearfully and wonderfully made; Marvelous are Your works, And that my soul knows very well."

Psalm 139:14

My daughter, Rebekah, is so creative. She makes unique jewelry for family and friends. I requested a set in green as a birthday gift. So, my daughter carefully selected every detail to make the necklace, bracelet, and earrings a special design. As each bead was delicately strung, it became a work of art that was truly gorgeous.

Touching the jewelry reminds me of Rebekah's diligent work. Each piece serves a purpose to make the jewelry practical, usable, and beautiful.

When I read Scripture, I'm reminded of how God made each of us unique with a special design and purpose. WOW!

✞ Marilyn

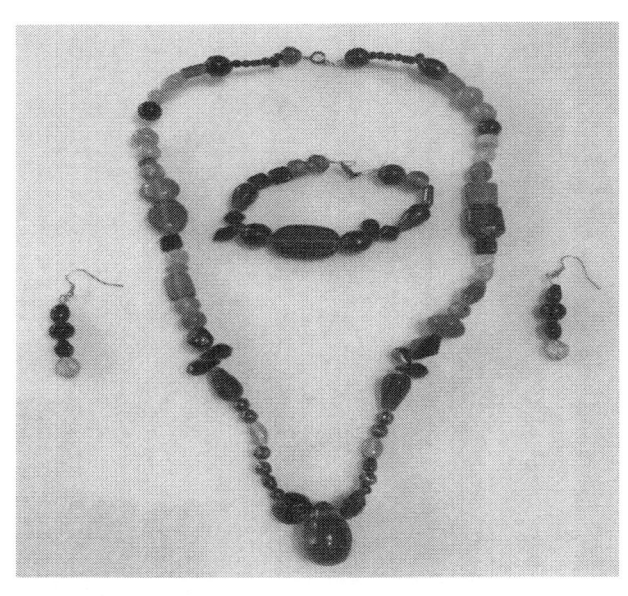

Jewelry Gems

1. What does it mean to be fearfully and wonderfully made?

_____
_____
_____
_____
_____
_____
_____

2. Read all of Chapter 2 of Ephesians. What does it mean that you were created to do good works? _____

_____
_____
_____
_____
_____

> "For we are His workmanship, created in Christ Jesus for good works, which God prepared beforehand that we should walk in them."
>
> *Ephesians 2:10*

Trinkets

"For as the body is one and has many members, but all the members of that one body, being many, are one body, so also is Christ."
I Corinthians 12:12

Have you ever looked for something that you knew you had but could not find? Perhaps it was an item of value to you alone representing part of your past. I recently experienced that exact scenario. I began rifling through drawers and small boxes scouring for an old piece of jewelry. In the process, I inspected several smaller containers within my jewelry box. Every receptacle was a different shape, size, one covered in velvet, one tiny and octagonal shaped, another long and narrow. Each held treasures inside from yesterdays. Although all containers were different, they were stored within the same piece of furniture that serves as my jewelry box.

While on the journey, the Lord began to speak to my heart.

- I was on a hunt for an item that held **significance** and a reminder of my past. God led me to read *Psalm 139*. He spoke to me gently, *"You are my significant treasure. Before the foundation of the world, I knew you and handcrafted you to radiate my glory."* Then God lead me to *I Peter 2:9*.

   "But you are a chosen generation, a royal priesthood, a holy nation, His own special people, that you may proclaim the praises of Him who called you out of darkness into His marvelous light."
   I Peter 2:9

- Pondering the first lesson, another soon surfaced. Many trinkets, through which I searched, were secured differently: boxes, tins, envelopes, and pockets. Regardless of how they were preserved, one large piece of furniture housed them all.

We, in the body of Christ, come packaged differently, and uniquely wrapped in physical appearance, ability, temperament, and personality. Yet, as His children, we are one in Him. We may each have different functions but when we work together, God is glorified and His name is lifted high.

Concluding my quest, I was rewarded. I found the piece of jewelry for which I had been searching! God has promised us many rewards. Our search, when directed by the Holy Spirit, always provides the best outcome. The most significant is eternal life.

✞ Sharon

Jewelry Gems

Perhaps you are a seeker. God invites you into His forever family. He stands at the door of your heart and knocks.

"Behold, I stand at the door and knock. If anyone hears My voice and opens the door, I will come in to him and dine with him, and he with Me."
Revelation 3:20

Record God's invitation and your response to Him._____

_____
_____
_____
_____
_____
_____
_____
_____
_____
_____
_____
_____
_____
_____

Dressed Appropriately

"Therefore take up the whole armor of God, that you may be able to withstand in the evil day, and having done all, to stand."
Ephesians 6:13

What can I say? I enjoy jewelry and need more than just a jewelry box. Oh, yes, it is a chest of drawers filled with treasures. I collected so many that even a large jewelry box wouldn't hold them. One side of the chest even has baskets with divided containers inside. Each holds matched sets of necklaces, earrings, and bracelets, so I can easily grab one of my favorites. Jewelry makes me feel dressed appropriately for any occasion.

Treasures have been purchased over the years and are carefully arranged for use. All silver jewelry is in one drawer, and I know where to find the pieces quickly. Gold items are in another. Sparkling rhinestones and fake diamonds are in a special container with a lid.

My expensive pieces: wedding pearls, diamond rings, and emeralds are secure in the bottom drawer. Each carefully wrapped for protection. When I need these items, they are not as easily assessable.

Planning is required to unpack items of great value and must be unwrapped to wear. There have been times when I have chosen other jewelry that is easy to grab even though it might not have been as appropriate for the event. The process to wear expensive items wasn't worth the time it took.

Not long ago, I couldn't find my Bible. Usually, I use my phone in church to read Scripture in Youversion. My phone is always with me, so it's easy to use. When writing, I look up several translations of Scripture using my phone. It's a time saver.

When I found my Bible, it was in a safe place. Like my expensive jewelry, my Bible was difficult to locate. I have a piece of furniture by the back door and my Bible was safe and secure on the bottom shelf.

Although it took effort to locate my Bible, I was thrilled to find it! Each page was filled with underlined Scriptures and handwritten notes from sermons and Bible studies. I felt prepared for the day with my Bible in hand.

How many times have I left my home without being appropriately prepared for the day? In *Ephesians 6:11-18*, we're instructed to dress for battle!

I decided it was worth it to start my day dressed appropriately. My Bible is next to the chair where I have morning devotions. I'll keep my phone in my purse and use my Bible to equip me for the day.

✝ Marilyn

Jewelry Gems

1. Read *Ephesians 6:14*. What does it mean to put on the breastplate of righteousness? _____

_____

_____

_____

_____

_____

2. Read *Ephesians 6:17*. What is the helmet of salvation? How can it be used? _____

_____

_____

_____

_____

3. How can you be dressed appropriately for battle? _____

_____

_____

_____

_____

_____

Surprised

"We can't afford it, you know that," Joe, my husband, said firmly.

"Please," I pleaded. "It can be birthday, Christmas, Valentine's and anniversary gift all combined in one."

"Quit asking for it!" Joe demanded. "How many people that are married do you see wearing their high school or college rings?"

"Lots, if they had a college ring as cool as the one I really really want," I lied. The conversation ended badly.

Crestfallen, and assured I wasn't getting the college ring; I gave up begging Joe for it. I knew we were dead broke. We had married when I was 20, in between my sophomore and junior year of college because he got drafted. It was a difficult time.

After being married for six weeks, he left for Viet Nam, and I only saw him for one week during the remainder of the first year of our marriage. Throughout that time, I went to college year-round and took as many classes as possible. I felt more like a widow than a wife. Upset, I rationalized that I deserved a college graduation ring, and I had the perfect one picked out. It was a pinkie ring with a little ruby for the Arkansas Razorbacks in the center. I was so disappointed I wasn't going to get it.

Much to my complete excitement, Joe surprised me with that ring I wanted so much. I really had given up hope I was going to get it, because truly, we had no money. Joe knew all along how much I wanted it and that he would find a way to make it happen.

God is a lot like that. He loves to give His children the desires of their hearts because He places the desires in our hearts to begin with. Sometimes, we don't get what we want because the timing isn't right. Maybe, God has something even better. Never believe God doesn't love to give you His best because … He does!

✞ Carolyn

Jewelry Gems

"If you then, being evil, know how to give good gifts to your children, how much more will your Father who is in heaven give good things to those who ask Him!"
Matthew 7:11

1. Write about a time you didn't get something you wanted only to discover God had planned something better for you.

_____

_____

_____

_____

2. Make a list of your blessings. Write a prayer thanking God for the good gifts He has given you. _____

_____

_____

_____

Charmed

"Apply your heart to instruction, And your ears to words of knowledge."
Proverbs 23:12

I was charmed by God's Word, both literally and figuratively, when I accepted an invitation to a Bible study thirty something years ago. Raised in a Christian home, I gave my heart to the Lord at a very young age. God blessed my life with many opportunities for spiritual growth. Yet, I struggled to know how to study the Bible for myself.

The invitation to B.S.F., Bible Study Fellowship, came at a critical period in my life. Struggling to raise a fourteen-year-old and starting over with a new baby was stretching my emotional endurance. I knew God's Word held the answers, however illusive it seemed. Void of time and lack of discipline, I was thirsty to go deeper with the Lord. However, that would mean I would have to find time to study God's Word. Desperate, I chose to begin a journey that changed my life.

Little by little, good habits were formed in me. Discipline in study and time management were the two biggest mountains to climb. While scaling the steep slopes, I began to hear and discern the voice of God. My prayer life grew deeper. With absolute confidence in God's love, it became easier to share my faith. Yet, He wasn't through stretching me. I was invited to take a leadership role. Now, it was no longer just about "me" but helping others to develop a love for God's Word. I am still reaping the benefits and sharing the lessons and tools with others.

The simple handcrafted sterling silver charm bracelet by Jeep Collins represents years of God's molding my life. The charms are a figurative reminder of the power of God's Word and its ability to change lives. Literally, the charms are a tangible symbol of the books studied while in B.S.F. The bracelet will always be a priceless keepsake for all the reasons mentioned and so much more.

✞ Sharon

Jewelry Gems

1. List ways in which God's Word has created a change in your life. _____

   _____

   _____

2. What has stunted you in your spiritual growth? List those areas where you feel inadequate. Use a concordance to help you find Scriptures and write them down. _____

   _____

   _____

   _____

3. In your spiritual walk, God will give you opportunities to be stretched. What is your response to the challenge? _____

   _____

   _____

Charms left to right: Genesis, Israel and the Minor Prophets, Matthew, Moses, John, Acts, Romans. Isaiah and Revelation are not shown.

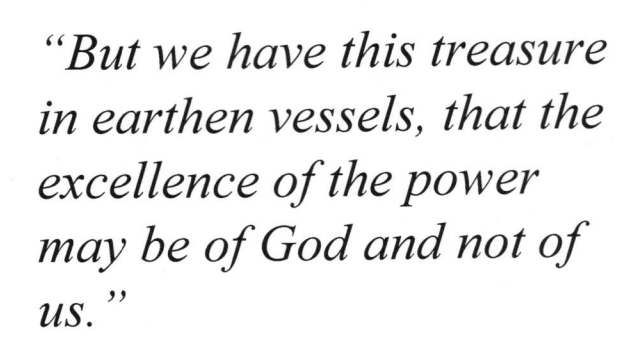

"But we have this treasure in earthen vessels, that the excellence of the power may be of God and not of us."

II Corinthians 4:7

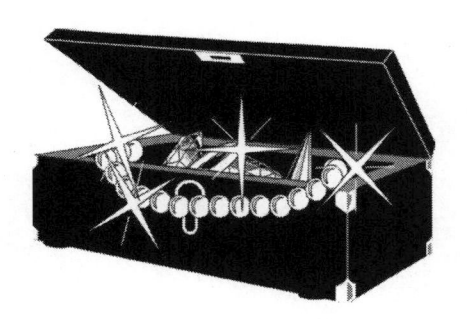

Chapter 12

To Teach About True Wealth

"Oh, the depth of the riches both of the wisdom and knowledge of God! How unsearchable are His judgments and His ways past finding out!"

Romans 11:33

Mom's Love Notes

My mom had the most beautiful engagement ring! It was a gold band with a gorgeous diamond. When we held hands, I always would want to touch her ring. Mom suffered from arthritis and her hands were swollen and painful. Eventually, she could no longer wear the treasured ring.

At age seventeen, I received an unexpected gift. Mom and Dad had the diamonds removed from her engagement ring. They were made into a necklace for me. I was overwhelmed with joy. Tears flowed. Along with the necklace was a handwritten note from Mom. I cherish this gift and will pass the necklace and note to my daughter.

The note and necklace are in my jewelry box. At age 94, Mom continues to handwrite notes with messages to me and our family. Each reminds me of how greatly I am loved. I treasure each note!

The Bible contains God's message. Scriptures give instruction, hope, and guidance. I'm so thankful for God's love notes!

✞ Marilyn

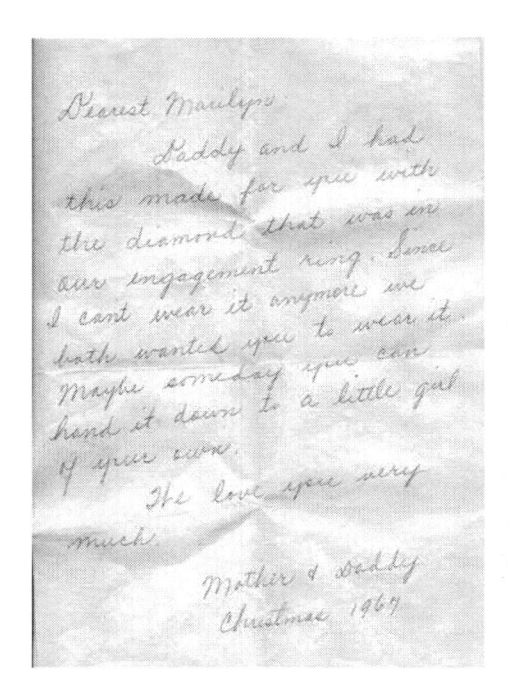

Jewelry Gems

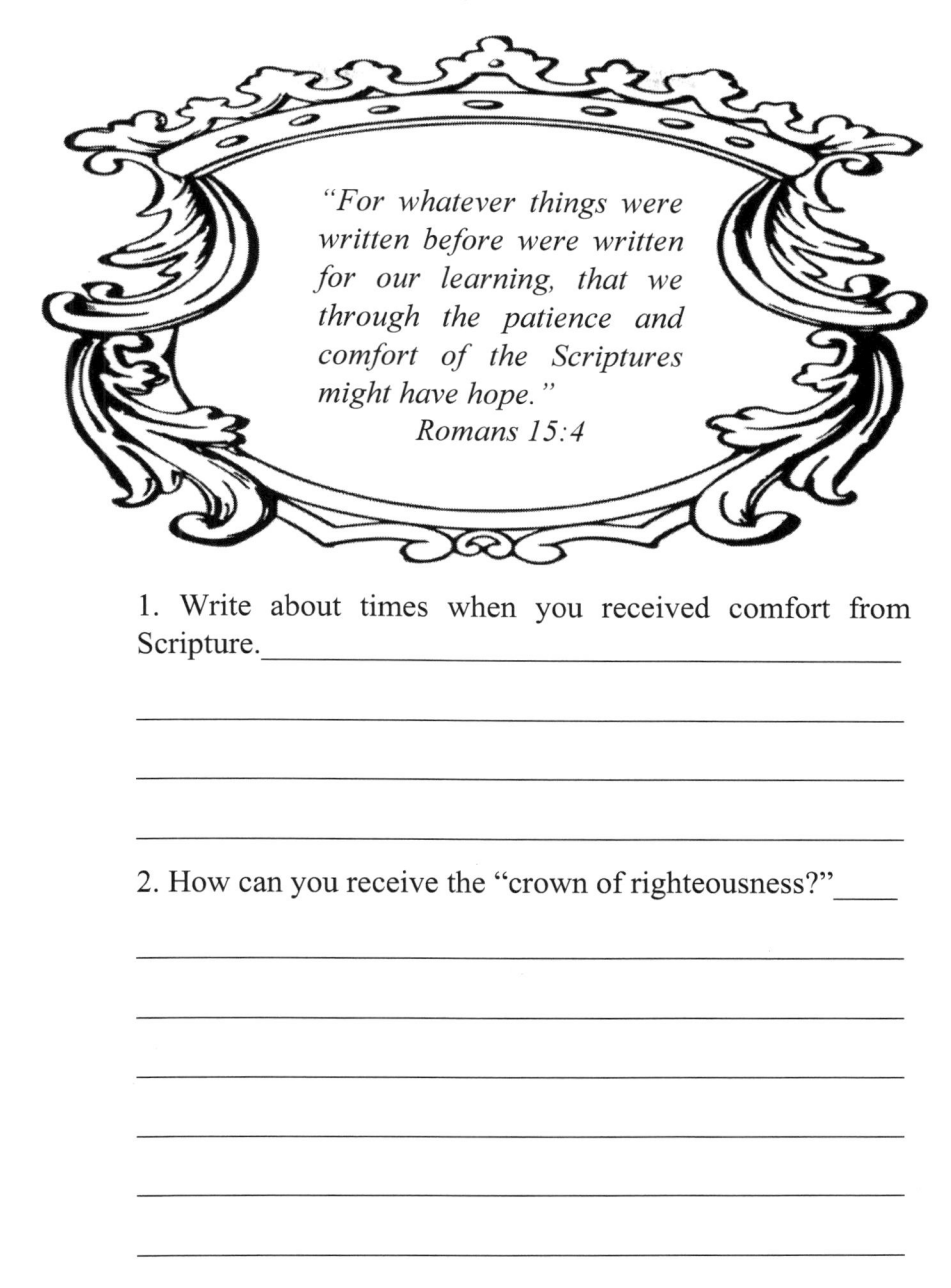

"For whatever things were written before were written for our learning, that we through the patience and comfort of the Scriptures might have hope."
Romans 15:4

1. Write about times when you received comfort from Scripture._____

_____

_____

_____

2. How can you receive the "crown of righteousness?"____

_____

_____

_____

_____

_____

_____

Triangle of Rubies and Pearls

My mom had this unique ring when I was growing up. It was a combination of pearls and rubies. Mom bought the ring when we lived in Japan. I called it a "Bogota" ring, but really I am not sure what the real name was. I just liked how that word rolled off my tongue. Since my mom has graduated to heaven, I received the ring from my dad. I wear it often. The shape of the ring reminds me of a little house.

Jesus taught a parable recorded in the book of Matthew. He talked about the difference between a wise man and a foolish one. Both built houses, but the difference was the type of ground they were built on. One built on rock, and the other was built on sinking sand. Christ is our foundation, for those who believe in Him. Ask for forgiveness of sins and live a life purposed for Him. Everything else is built on sinking sand.

✞ Terri

Jewelry Gems

"Therefore whoever hears these sayings of Mine, and does them, I will liken him to a wise man who built his house on the rock: and the rain descended, the floods came, and the winds blew and beat on that house; and it did not fall, for it was founded on the rock. But everyone who hears these sayings of Mine, and does not do them, will be like a foolish man who built his house on the sand: and the rain descended, the floods came, and the winds blew and beat on that house; and it fell. And great was its fall."
Matthew 7:24-27

1. What do you need to give up or turn from in order to shore up your foundation? Examples are: T.V. shows, social media, or the latest app for your electronics. _____

_____

_____

_____

2. Pray for an accountability partner to keep you in check. Choose someone who will be truthful, honest, helpful, and kind. We all need someone to do this for us. Who might this person be? _____

_____

_____

_____

_____

Rich

Kids notice more than you might think. I taught middle school for twenty years. Often my sixth graders would comment about my hair, clothes, or jewelry. If anything was different about me, they noticed and shared their opinions. Occasionally, I wore a costume necklace that had a very large "diamond" surrounded by "gold." Invariably every time I wore it, several students asked, "Mrs. Hedgecock, is that a real diamond in your necklace?"

In my mind I thought, *Seriously, do you think I'd be teaching if I owned a million dollar diamond? And do you really think I'd wear million dollar jewelry to school?* Of course, I kept my thoughts private and always gave the same response, "Do you think I'd wear anything that wasn't real?"

Most students replied, "No, wow, Mrs. Hedgecock you must be really rich!"

I'd chuckle to myself and think, *Yes, I really am rich, but not in the way you think. I'm rich because I have a job I love, students I love, a beautiful home and family; but most importantly, I'm rich because I have the Lord in my life.*

☩ Carolyn

Jewelry Gems

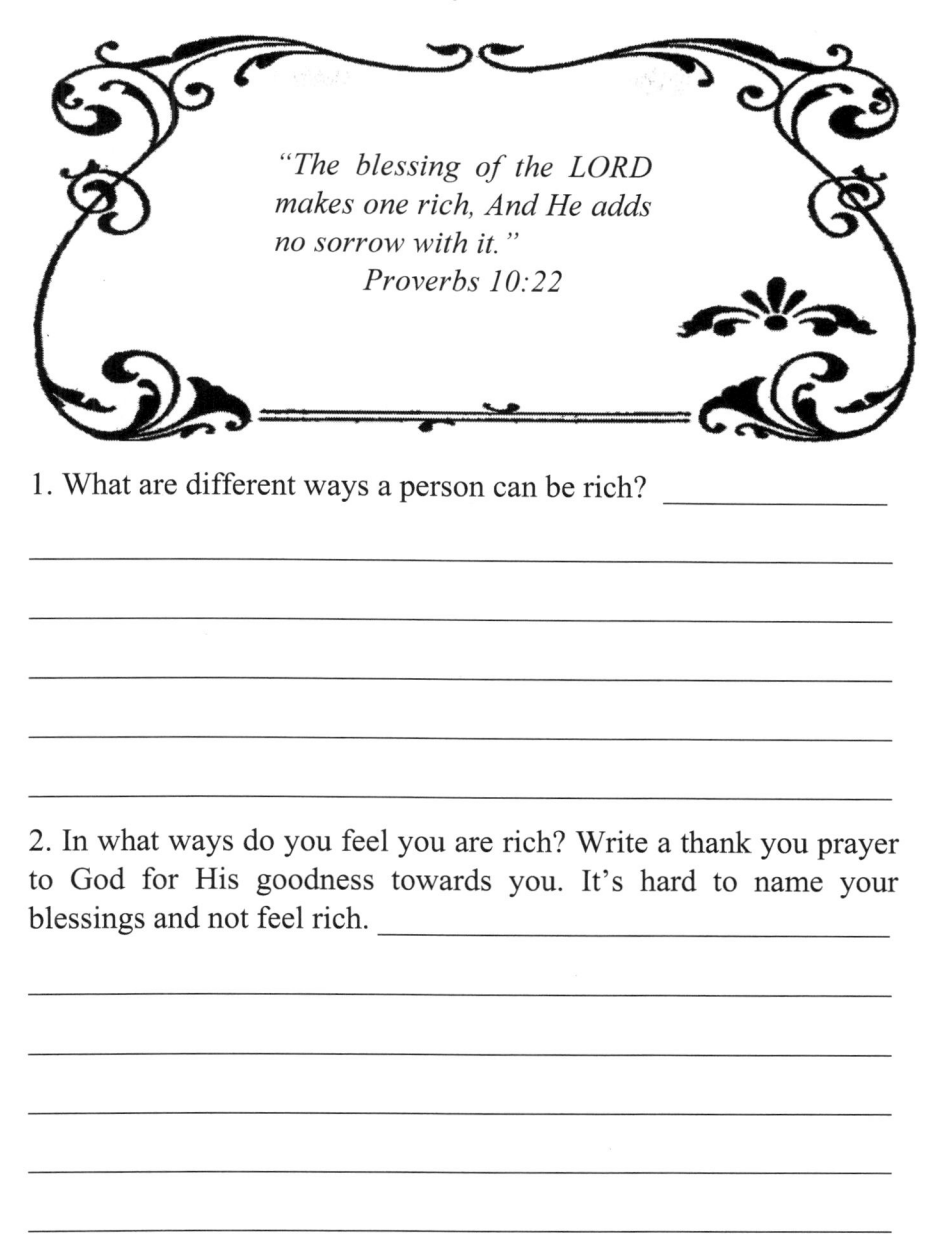

"The blessing of the LORD makes one rich, And He adds no sorrow with it."
Proverbs 10:22

1. What are different ways a person can be rich? _____

_____

_____

_____

_____

2. In what ways do you feel you are rich? Write a thank you prayer to God for His goodness towards you. It's hard to name your blessings and not feel rich. _____

_____

_____

_____

_____

_____

"Gramma" Treasures

While shopping, I walked past a man wearing a shirt with this caption: "If I had known having grandchildren was this much fun, I would have had them first!" That made my day!

My three daughters have blessed me with seven wonderful grandchildren: five boys and two girls. I remember when Nathaniel was born. He was the first boy on my side of the family in 76 years!

My youngest daughter was boasting that she finally did something first, that is, before her two older sisters, ha. Then, she did it again and had the second boy, Benjamin. Five days after he was born, Zoë made her appearance. We call them "twin cousins." Then all three daughters had a child the same school year: Jenaya, Zachary and Caedmon. The last to arrive was Malachi. Our quivers were full.

The grandma jewelry was given to me with smiles, giggles, hugs, and kisses. The four little grandchildren charms are so cute! All the sparkling birthstones are so cheerful. As I muse over these, I wonder where the time has gone. Nathaniel just turned 18 and graduates this May. Ben and Zoë are 16. Jenaya and Zachary are 13 with Caedmon soon to be 13. Malachi will be 11. As they say, "such is life."

Although I love my grandchildren with all my heart, the one thing that thrills me most is that all seven are saved! They have asked Jesus into their hearts! We will be together forever.

Our Father God thinks in generations. He is known as the God of Abraham, Isaac, and Jacob. The Bible says God chose Abraham because He knew he would teach his children the oracles of God.

♪Linda

Jewelry Gems

"And I will establish My covenant between Me and you and your descendants after you in their generations, for an everlasting covenant, to be God to you and your descendants after you."
Genesis 17:7

1. How is God generational? What does that mean to you?

_____

_____

_____

_____

2. How can you be an example to your children and grandchildren to draw them into God's presence?

_____

_____

3. What can you do to provide opportunities for your family to grow in the Lord? _____

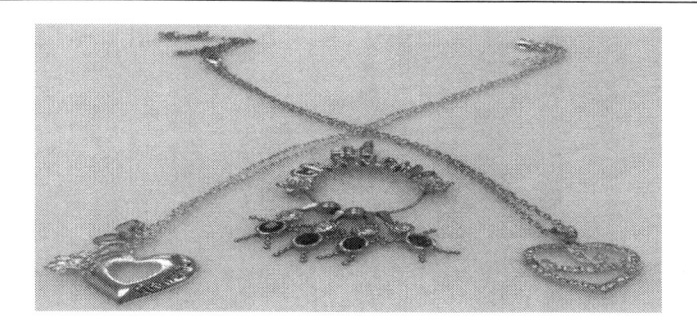

_____

_____

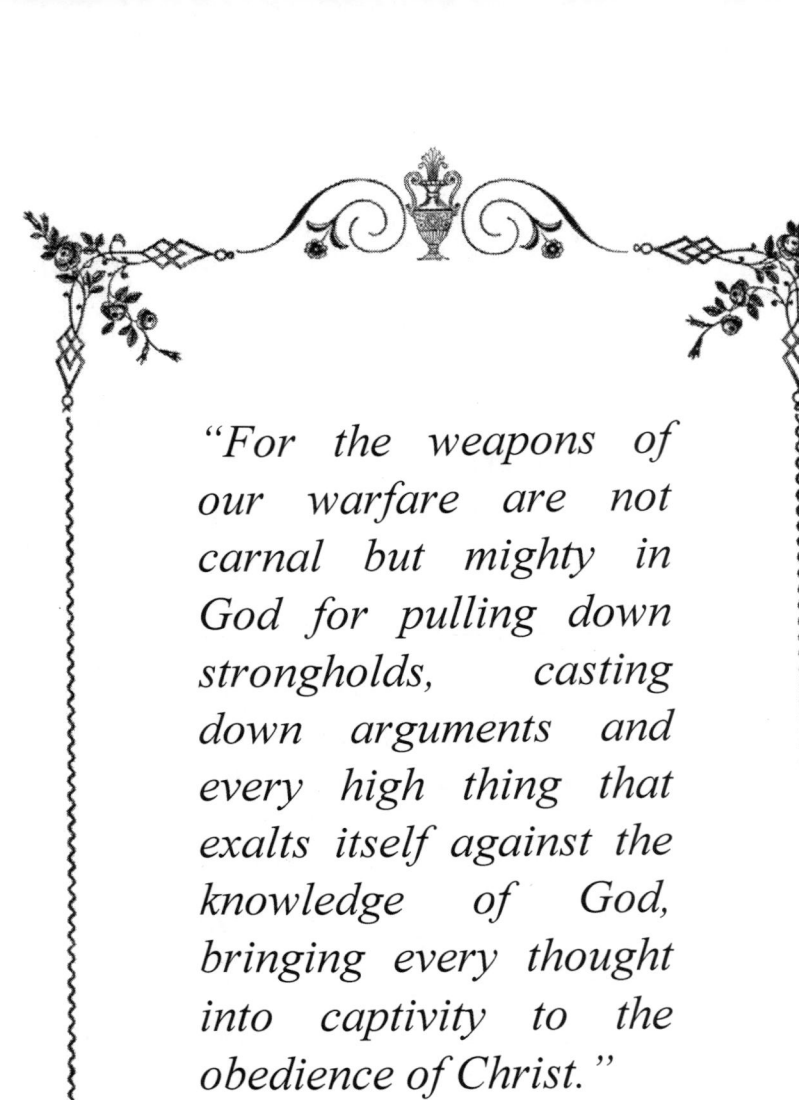

"For the weapons of our warfare are not carnal but mighty in God for pulling down strongholds, casting down arguments and every high thing that exalts itself against the knowledge of God, bringing every thought into captivity to the obedience of Christ."

11 Corinthians 10:4-5

Chapter 13

To Use During Spiritual Battles

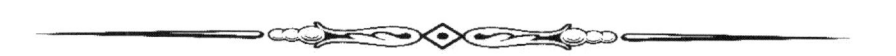

"Yet in all these things we are more than conquerors through Him who loved us."

Romans 8:37

Mighty Warrior

My friend, I don't know what kind of battle you might be fighting. Spiritual warfare is real. If you are a child of God, be prepared because attacks will come. However, here's some good news; there is victory when you approach problems with Scripture and prayer.

I know this statement might sound melodramatic, but a simple necklace helped me through one of my darkest times. Without going into specifics, I became bombarded at home and work by unexpected out-of-my-control situations. Doubts and fears attacked me like unwanted intruders.

Usually I started my day with a brief quiet time, but then I would get to school and life began. While teaching around 150 sixth graders, I couldn't say, "Hey kids, could you just chill a few minutes while I pray and read my Bible?" I asked God for something to help me stand firm and open my eyes to know He was my mighty warrior, there to help, in every situation. Before I left home, I usually wrote Scripture on index cards and carried them around with me like a sweet blanket. They gave me comfort, but one Saturday afternoon at a mall I found a gold mine, actually it was more like a silver lode.

Walking through the jewelry section in a department store, my eye was drawn to a silver necklace shaped like a small box. Getting closer, I began reading the inscription and wept. It was *Psalm 37:24* and said, *"Though he fall, he shall not be utterly cast down; for the Lord upholds him with His hand."* Immediately, I bought it.

When doubts and fears tried to high-jack my faith, I would grab my necklace and rub it between my thumb and index fingers. I rubbed that necklace so much that some of the words have become faint. Holding it, I would imagine the Lord directly saying to me, *Carolyn, I've got you and I'm not going to let you fall. You will get through this.* That became my truth which was bound around my neck and mind.

✝ Carolyn

Jewelry Gems

"Let not mercy and truth forsake you; Bind them around your neck. Write them on the tablet of your heart."
Proverbs 3:3

1. Write *Ephesians 6:10-20* in your own words. _____

_____

_____

_____

2. Read *Ephesians 6:10-20*. What specific instructions are given for a child of God? _____

_____

_____

_____

3. What are some of Satan's tactics to keep you blind to warfare?

_____

_____

_____

_____

Three Strands Strong

"Though one may be overpowered by another, two can withstand him. And a threefold cord is not quickly broken."
Ecclesiastes 4:12

I have three strands of pearls that have a multicolored clasp flower with matching earrings. I really like the necklace and the way I feel when wearing it. I know that is a bit silly, but there are certain things we wear that make us feel special and ... this is one of those things.

When we decide to become a follower of Christ and invite Him into our life as Savior and Lord, we become part of that threefold cord.

The moment a decision is made for Christ, we receive the Holy Spirit who dwells within us to be our helper and guide. Then, we gain a heavenly Father God to talk to and lean on. He is a Father who wants to bless us and give us wisdom and understanding. All we have to do is ask. Our threefold cord is Jesus, the Holy Spirit, and God.

✟ Terri

Jewelry Gems

1. What are you looking for in the way of understanding? _____

_____
_____
_____
_____
_____

2. Write about a situation where you need wisdom. _____

_____
_____
_____
_____
_____

3. Write a prayer for your request. _____

_____
_____
_____
_____
_____
_____
_____
_____

Angels All Around

"For He shall give His angels charge over you, To keep you in all your ways."
Psalm 91:11

The desire of all holy angels is to honor God. When the G.A.L.S. wear angel jewelry, that is our motivation as well. We found some beautiful angel bracelets and necklaces we enjoy wearing while we prepared for a program about "God's messengers."

As we researched, we discovered there are over 270 references of angels in the Bible; 108 are in the Old Testament and 165 are in the New Testament. Never to be worshipped, angels can do nothing apart from God.

When we wear our angel jewelry, we imagine what heaven is like when people get saved. The Bible tells us angels celebrate. Worshipping and praising God are the main functions of angels. Also, they deliver messages, protect, lead the way, instruct, guide, communicate understanding, forewarn, quiet, and comfort.

Did you know you have your own guardian angel assigned specifically to you? Each holy angel has a special unique assignment as different as snowflakes. According to *Hebrew 1:14*, Angel armies are on high alert and respond to God's will. Some are assigned to battle spiritual warfare. They are dispersed to defend and protect individuals and families.

Attacks on you or your family may come from discouragement, disappointments, rebellion, separations, divisions, or distortions of truth. Whenever personal or family assaults occur, put on your armor and perhaps angel jewelry to remind you the spirit beings are loyal servants of God who have supernatural powers. Ask God to activate His angels to fight on your behalf.

✞ God's Amazing Love Storytellers

Jewelry Gems

1. Read *Hebrews 13:2*. Write what it means to you. _____

_____

_____

_____

2. Write *Psalms 103:20* in your own words. _____

_____

_____

_____

"And His kingdom rules over all. Bless the LORD, you His angels, Who excel in strength, who do His word, Heeding the voice of His word."
                    Psalms 103:19-20

G.A.L.S. always wear jewelry that tells a story. One of our favorite bracelets is a silver angel. It reminds us that angels are on high alert to minister.

"Let us hold fast the confession of our hope without wavering, for He who promised is faithful."

Hebrews 10:23-24

Chapter 14

To Ask God to Order My Steps

"The steps of a good man are ordered by the Lord, And He delights in his way."

Psalm 37:23

Flip Flops

Going to Hawaii was a dream vacation for my husband and me a few years ago. Everything about it was fun. Strolling on the beach at dusk with my sweetheart was something I especially enjoyed. Joe knows how much I love jewelry. On most trips, he lets me pick out a piece as a souvenir. Little flip flop necklaces were sold at practically every tourist shop. They came in all different colors, were inexpensive, and fun to wear.

I got a turquoise flip flop necklace that said, "Hawaii" on it. When I saw the necklace relaxing in my jewelry box, it took me back to walks on the beach. Also, it drew me to a Scripture I have framed in my house. *Psalm 37:23* says, *"The steps of a good man are ordered by the Lord and He delights in his way."*

Whenever you see shoes of your loved ones lying around the house, don't get upset because they were left out. Instead, pray for the loved ones they belong to. Ask God to order the steps of your spouse, children and/or grandchildren. Also, ask God to order your steps. Look for connections to draw you to the Lord with every piece of jewelry in your jewelry box. Once you get started, you will flip with excitement and not want to stop.

✞ Carolyn

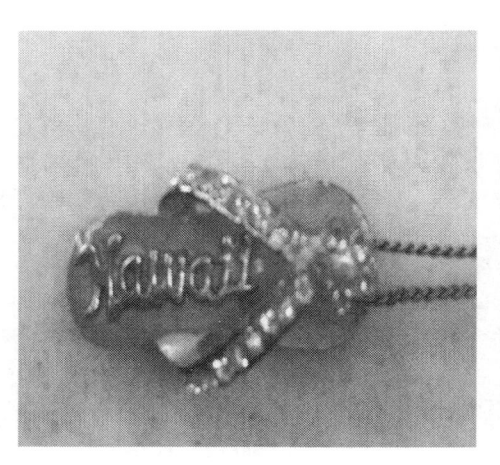

Jewelry Gems

"A man's heart plans his way, but the Lord directs his steps."
Proverbs 16:9

1. List ways the Lord has ordered your steps. Have you ever had a divine appointment where the Lord connected you with just the right person you needed in your life at just the exact time? Write about it. _____

_____

_____

_____

_____

2. Write a prayer asking the Lord to direct the steps of one of your loved ones. Be specific. Thank Him in advance for His faithfulness.

_____

_____

_____

_____

3. Read *Proverbs 13:20*. Write your thoughts. _____

_____

_____

_____

_____

Watches and Time

Watches, all broken but still secure in a drawer, keep me aware of time, days already lived. Two pieces are merely sentimental in value. One belonged to my dad. All that is left of his watch is the dirty face under the cracked crystal with no band. He wore the watch every day for most of my life.

One distinct memory I have of my dad wearing the watch was the day he jumped into a swiftly flowing canal to rescue me and my brother. The watch although totally submerged continued to keep perfect time for many more years.

The other is my mother's watch. It quit working long before she quit wearing it. A gift from a cherished group of friends, she held on to the watch not wanting to ever forget the friendships it represented. My mother was a practical woman and enjoyed few accessories. Although I am not sure she ever looked at it, she wore it whenever she left the house. She was not time conscience, but rather people aware. Her watch was merely perfunctory.

Although watches are not mentioned in Scripture ... TIME is mentioned at least 710 instances. With so many references to time it must be important. Time is not an item for which we can bargain. It is perishable and irreplaceable. God in His grace, has given us all the same amount, 24 hours per day. The quality, joy, and impact of our lives are directly related to how wisely we use the time we have.

✝ Sharon

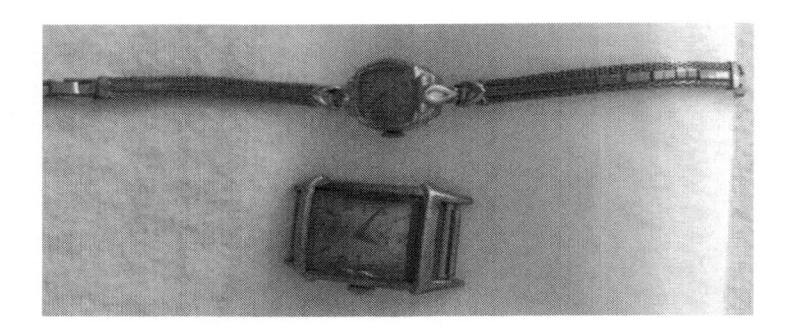

Jewelry Gems

> *"And He said to them, "It is not for you to know times or seasons which the Father has put in His own authority."*
> *Acts 1:7*

1. What is your view of time? How does it relate to God's plan for your life? _____

_____

_____

_____

_____

_____

_____

2. Yesterday is gone and you cannot get it back. Tomorrow may come, but you have no guarantees; so, that leaves today. Invite God to order your day. What are some thoughts He has given you about how to use today? Write them down and check off each item when completed. _____

_____

_____

_____

_____

_____

_____

Cut and Molded

"But now, O LORD, you are our Father; We are the clay, You are our potter; And we are the work of Your hand."
Isaiah 64:8

Have you thought about the process of making a ring? If you've ever had the opportunity to watch a craftsman at work, it is amazing. The way the master works the material to create the piece of art is really awe-inspiring. First, artists determine what they want to create by designing the item. Then, the fabrication process begins. The steel is prepared and cut, then heated to bend all to create the piece of art. The final product is polished to complete the process.

God, the creator of the universe, is the master craftsman. We are the clay in His mighty hands being worked to become more like Him with every passing day, every trial that comes our way, or every situation that arises. The final product of our life comes when we get to go home to heaven. It is then, we will be made perfect in Him.

✝ Terri

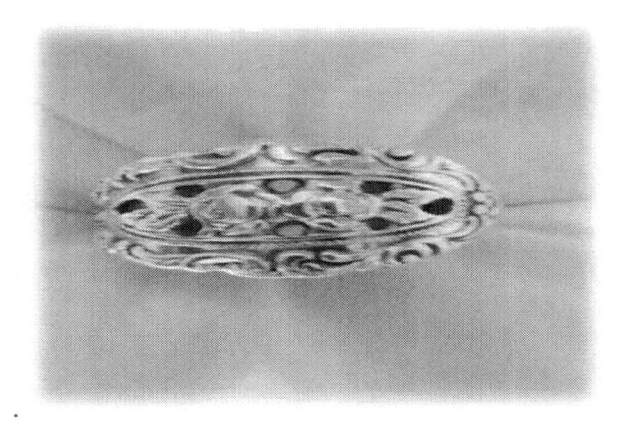

Jewelry Gems

1. What are areas in your life where you need God's help? _____

_____
_____
_____
_____
_____
_____
_____
_____

2. Write a prayer praising God for being the master craftsman in your life. _____

_____
_____
_____
_____
_____
_____
_____
_____
_____

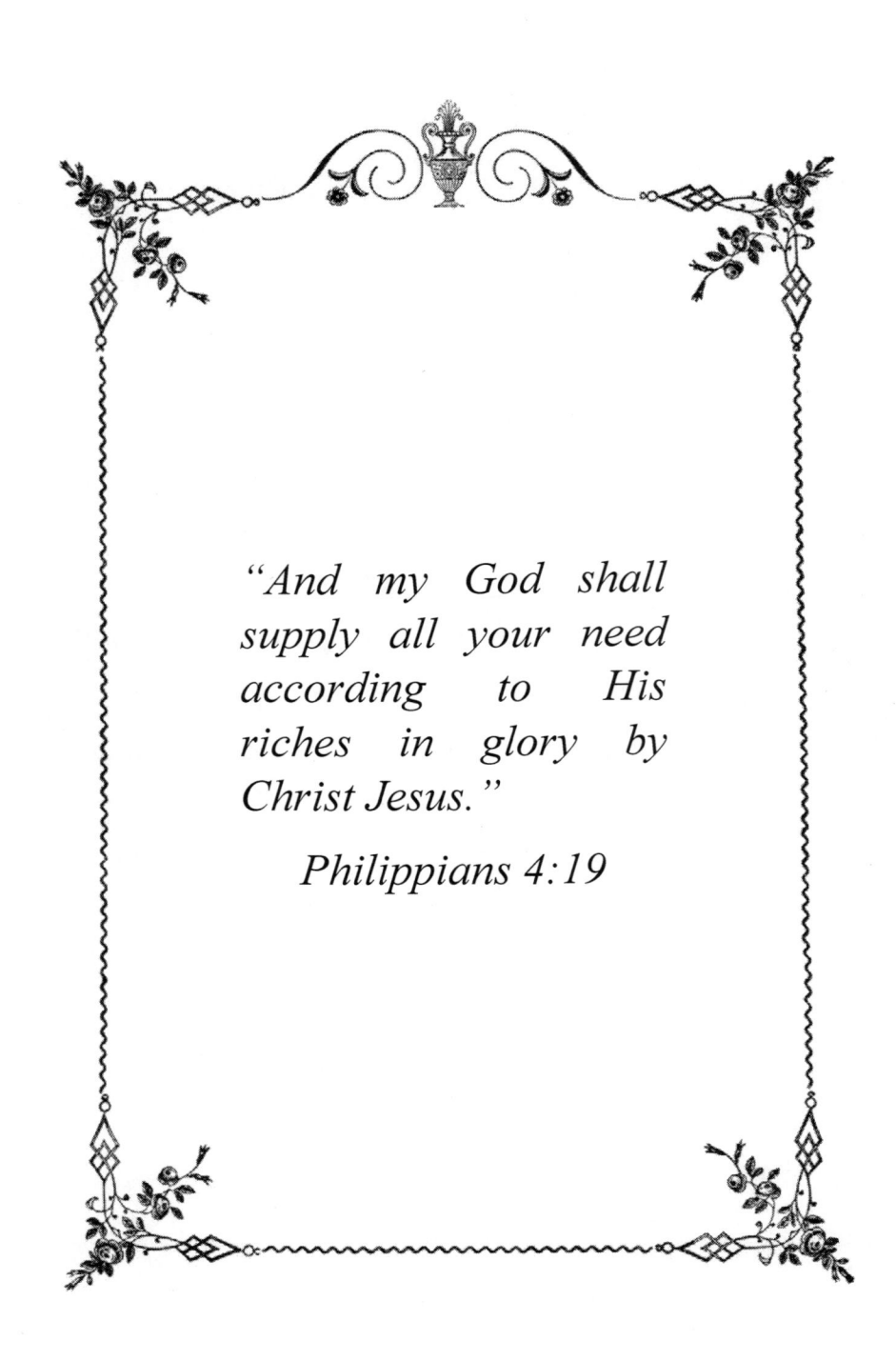

"And my God shall supply all your need according to His riches in glory by Christ Jesus."

Philippians 4:19

Chapter 15

To Build Up Faith in Believers

"These things I have written to you who believe in the name of the Son of God, that you may know that you have eternal life, and that you may continue to believe in the name of the Son of God."

I John 5:13

Faith, Hope, Love

A James Avery bracelet that was a gift from my sister, Sharron, and my brother, Randy, for my 50th birthday is one of my favorite pieces of jewelry. My brother and sister and I often meet for lunch and pray for one another. We have prayed together through numerous difficult life situations. When I wear the bracelet, I'm consistently reminded of God's promises in the Bible!

The confident assurance of faith in my life has given hope in God through many of life's most difficult situations! I'm so thankful for God's amazing love!

✞ Marilyn

Faith - *"Now **faith** is the substance of things hoped for, the evidence of things not seen." Hebrews 11:1*

Hope - *"Now may the God of **hope** fill you with all joy and peace in believing, that you may abound in **hope** by the power of the Holy Spirit." Romans 15:13*

Love - *"Who shall separate us from the **love** of Christ? Shall tribulation, or distress, or persecution, or famine, or nakedness, or peril, or sword?" Romans 8:35*

Jewelry Gems

1. What is faith according to the Bible? _____
   _____
   _____

2. Write about a time when God used faith to help you through a difficult situation. _____
   _____
   _____

3. What is a definition of hope according to the Bible? _____
   _____
   _____

3. What does *I Corinthians 13:13* mean to you? _____
   _____
   _____
   _____

> *"And now abide faith, hope, love, these three; but the greatest of these is love."*
>
> I Corinthians 13:13

Quick Fix

Our generation wants quick solutions to all problems. Living in a hurried world, we want everything done yesterday, but God seldom works like that.

Waiting is not fun. You've probably heard the saying, "Haste makes waste." When I've thought God's timing was too slow or never going to happen, I have taken matters in my own hands. Enormous messes followed which seemed beyond repair.

On a vacation, I found a necklace which reminded me that God can take broken pieces and turn them into something new and beautiful. The necklace, made up of lots of tiny diamond discards, was expensive. A crafty jeweler gathered many miniscule diamonds too small to be useable individually. He must have spent hours putting the tiny sparkly fragments into the necklace. With time and skill, all the broken diamonds were transformed into a thing of beauty.

God is the master jeweler of people. At first glance, undesirable situations and people might seem like they should fall into a hopeless category. But here is the good news, **Nothing is impossible with God.** In fact, He is always up for a challenge. Be amazed when you ask Him to turn beauty from ashes. Pray for God to turn the messes of your life into His treasured masterpieces. There is only one catch ... you must give Him **all** your broken pieces.

✞ Carolyn

Jewelry Gems

"Behold, the LORD's hand is not shortened, that it cannot save; nor His ear heavy, that it cannot hear."
Isaiah 59:1

1. Write a statement of faith and truth based on *Isaiah 59:1* concerning a situation or person in your life that needs an intervention from God. Be specific. _____

_____

_____

_____

_____

2. Read *Ephesians 1:17-20*. What is the glory of His inheritance for His saints? _____

_____

_____

_____

_____

_____

_____

_____

_____

_____

_____

Trumpet

Many years have passed since I first picked up my cornet. It is essentially identical to a trumpet: the difference being that is it a little shorter and has a more cone-shaped bell. My family moved three times during my high school years to Oklahoma, Texas, and New Mexico.

It is usually difficult for a teen to fit in with the local groups, but God helped me by giving me a gift in music. I scored ones in state solo/ensemble contests and actually made it to the Texas All State Band and later the New Mexico All-Region Band.

I had a partial scholarship to U.N.M. and played in the band for a year. As time went on, I married and had three daughters. We moved back to Texas. As the Lord directed, I was able to return to school and earn a Bachelor of Science in Music Education from Texas Woman's University. First trumpet in the jazz band, I played my senior recital on this same cornet.

Somewhere in the music mix, after playing the organ in church for seven years, the opportunity came to play my cornet in church. The Lord began teaching me how to "blow the trumpet in Zion." That was a GLORIOUS season! This precious horn finally wore out. It sits in a case enshrining many memories.

Now, I sing and play the piano and keyboard at church. In G.A.L.S., I am the praise dancer and even get to write and take part in drama/skits and video projects! God is using us to build an orphanage in Africa called G.A.L.S.O.! How awesome is that!!! God has been, and continues to be, so good to me. I love Him with my whole heart.

I share my cornet story because the Lord wants to encourage you and to stir up the gift He has deposited within you. As you walk with the Lord, He will anoint you to blow your "trumpet" in Zion. Maybe you are a seamstress, writer, dancer, intercessor, teacher, caregiver, doctor, nurse, secretary, educator, parent, grandparent, computer programmer, photographer, business owner, entrepreneur, etc. Invite Jesus to be the C.E.O. of your life. Put on your seatbelt. You are in for a GLORIOUS ride! Let's face it, as Scripture tells us, Jehovah is coming. We have the great honor and responsibility of sounding that message to everyone we can.

It is never too late to join the team. Our Father God will help us throw off the shackles, if need be, and put on His armor. Read *Ephesians 6*. No one should miss heaven! Blow <u>YE</u> the trumpet in Zion!

♪Linda

Jewelry Gems

"Blow the trumpet in Zion, And sound an alarm in My holy mountain! Let all the inhabitants of the land tremble; For the day of the Lord is coming, For it is at hand."
Joel 2:1

1. Describe a piece of jewelry that you have which brings life-time memories. _____

_____

_____

_____

2. What does it mean for you to "blow the trumpet in Zion?" Do you need to ask Jesus to be your C.E.O.? _____

_____

_____

_____

_____

3. Who can you partner with to use your gifts in helping to populate heaven? Ask the Lord, He knows! _____

_____

_____

_____

_____

_____

_____

Chapter 16

To Explore the Power of Praise

"I will praise You, O LORD, with my whole heart; I will tell of all Your marvelous works."

Psalm 9:1

Lead Me to the Rock

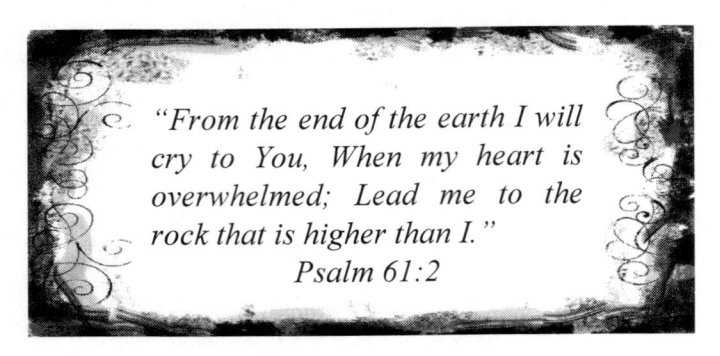

> *"From the end of the earth I will cry to You, When my heart is overwhelmed; Lead me to the rock that is higher than I."*
> Psalm 61:2

Isn't it funny what we keep as treasures? Most of the little items that have meant so much to me over the years end up in my jewelry catalog.

I ran across a rock that Marilyn gave the G.A.L.S. several years ago. The Scripture on the rock from *Psalm 61:2* reads, *"Lead me to the rock that is higher than I."* At the time she gave this to us, her daughter was in the hospital very ill. When I pulled it out of one of the drawers, I rolled the rock around in my hand for a few minutes. I thought of Marilyn, Nolan, and Rebekah and how often they have looked to the One who is higher than they.

Grateful that God has allowed me the privilege of their friendship, I watch with amazement as they lead others to the rock through their demonstration of faith.

✞ Sharon

Jewelry Gems

Although I have not had the same struggles, I too am dependent on the One who is higher than I. What about you? To whom do you run when life's storms are raging?

Write down your greatest struggles. Now thank God for helping you through each one. Praise Him that He has secured your steps.

_____
_____
_____
_____
_____
_____
_____
_____
_____
_____
_____
_____
_____
_____
_____
_____
_____

A New Song

"The LORD is my strength and song, And He has become my salvation."

Exodus 15:2a

When I was a young girl, my mom gave me a pretty silver necklace and earrings set that had dainty little music notes attached. Simply beautiful! Mom reminded me that I have a new song in my heart because I made the decision to have Jesus be the leader of my life. At that time those words had meaning, but ... now as an adult looking back those words have such a deeper chord.

As a little girl, the Lord was my strength and song and became my salvation through my decision to trust Him. *Exodus 15:2* goes on to say, *"He is my God, and I will praise Him."* Through the ups and downs of life, I know He is my God and deserves all my praise!

It has taken a lifetime of joys along with sorrows to come to the realization. When I made that decision as a young child, at that very moment in time Jesus did become my salvation. I began to walk with Him that day, one that was meant to be a lifelong journey. I began a personal relationship with Jesus. The word "personal" in and of itself demands attention to the details of knowing someone.

As I grew in Him through Bible study and learned about Jesus, He became my salvation, the rock on which I hold everything dear. Jesus is the song in my heart! He is the voice of praise my mouth sings about! I have undergone a change because of "whose" child I am! I have a new song in my heart because of Jesus!

✝ Terri

Jewelry Gems

Have you made the decision to have a personal relationship with Jesus? If not, and you would like to do so right now, turn to page 198-201. This will give you a simple explanation and provides a prayer to follow. There is a place to put today's date as well. The next thing you need to do is go tell someone! Such an exciting decision needs to be shared with people, your family, friends, co-workers, everyone who will listen to what you have to say. When you make this decision, you are in the most unique place to be, changed for all eternity; now part of the family of God! You have a new song in your heart today, this very instance! There is an old hymn called the Doxology from that says these words: "Praise God, from whom all blessings flow; Praise Him, all creatures here below; Praise Him above, ye heav'nly host; Praise Father, Son, and Holy Ghost. Amen." Doxology (Words by Thomas Ken, 1695)

Find a new song for your heart to sing. In the place below write a song of praise to God for what He has done for you. _____

_____

_____

_____

_____

_____

_____

_____

_____

Jesus is the Reason

Christmas season is filled with decorating, shopping, gift exchanges, parties, church activities, family gatherings, and cooking. It's so easy to get caught up in the busyness of activities. Often, the true reason for the season is forgotten.

The birth of Christ is the significant event that brings meaning to Christmas. We focus on displaying the manger scene and reading Bible verses about the birth of our Savior in December. But there's so much more!

Isn't Jesus the Reason for everything we celebrate as Christians: new life in Christ, forgiveness, and living for eternity in the presence of God?

When I wear my Christmas earrings, they give me an opportunity to share about Jesus! People seem so receptive in December.

Perhaps we should focus on Jesus every calendar day as well! Jesus is the reason we celebrate Christmas, but also the reason for all seasons: spring, summer, fall, and winter.

✞ Marilyn

Jewelry Gems

"For there is born to you this day in the city of David a Savior, who is Christ the Lord. And this will be the sign to you: You will find a Babe wrapped in swaddling cloths, lying in a manger."
Luke 2:11-12

1. List things that you do at Christmas to celebrate the birth of Jesus Christ. _____

_____

_____

_____

2. How can you celebrate Jesus every day of the year? _____

_____

_____

_____

_____

3. How can you keep Christ in Christmas during all the busyness?

_____

_____

_____

_____

_____

_____

_____

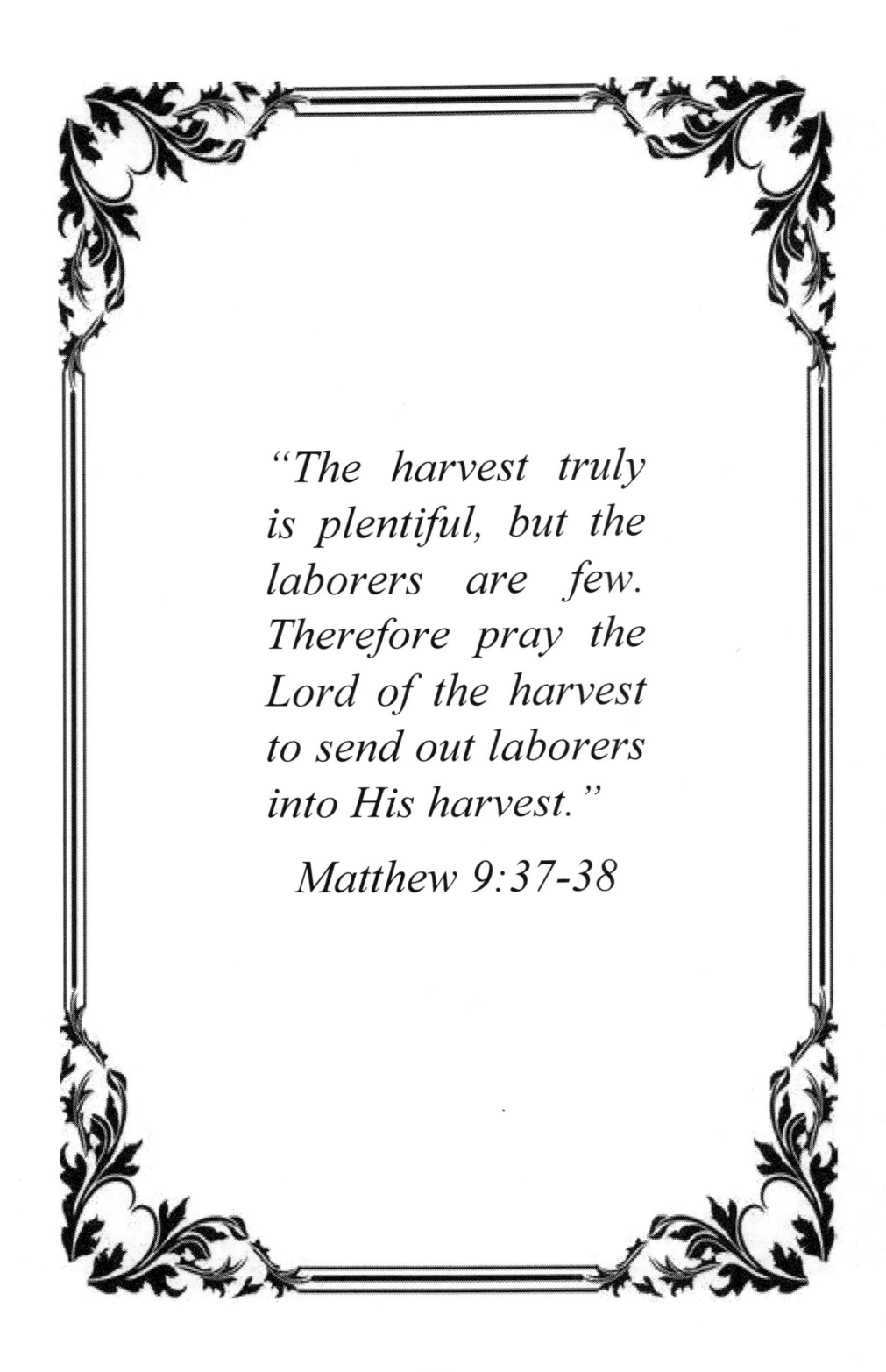

"The harvest truly is plentiful, but the laborers are few. Therefore pray the Lord of the harvest to send out laborers into His harvest."

Matthew 9:37-38

Chapter 17

To Open Doors to Share God's Love

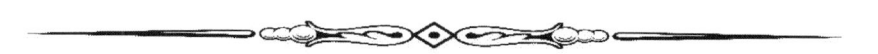

"The LORD your God in your midst, The Mighty One, will save; He will rejoice over you with gladness, He will quiet you in His love, He will rejoice over you with singing."

Zephaniah 3:17

Duel Blessing

Some time ago, I was part of a ministry for ladies which made a special logo charm for a necklace. Designed by our leader, who is now in Heaven, it had diamonds in a unique setting.

At a conference, one of the invited ministers really liked my necklace. She commented about it each of the three days. I was prompted to give her the necklace. To my surprise, she gave me the necklace she was wearing.

As we shared our hearts, it was a duel blessing for both of us. The necklace she gave me had a pearl cross on one side and a cross of small clustered diamonds on the other, another duel blessing!

That necklace is one of my favorites. It reminds me of how we need each other and have pearls of wisdom to share. It also reminds me of the ways Jesus touches and heals lives.

We can learn from each other as mothers and daughters who explore and search for the jewels and nuggets in the Word of God.

♪Linda

Jewelry Gems

1. How can you find a group of ladies in which you can share Jesus, be encouraged, and offer encouragement? _____

_____

_____

2. Write about a teaching you received that was meaningful to you.

_____

_____

_____

_____

When reading this Scripture, you can insert "daughter" for son.

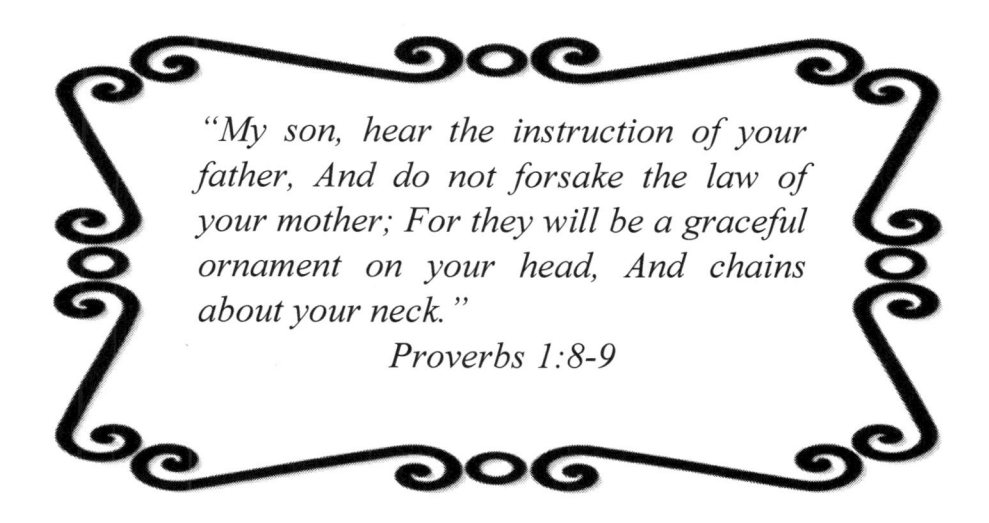

> *"My son, hear the instruction of your father, And do not forsake the law of your mother; For they will be a graceful ornament on your head, And chains about your neck."*
> *Proverbs 1:8-9*

Ten Commandments

The Ten Commandments are a key to understanding the Old Testament and the ministry of Jesus. God's moral standard shows us how Christians should live. It may seem impossible to keep them, but we have a God who forgives and helps us daily. I have a bracelet that reminds me.

The Ten Commandments are found in *Exodus 20:1–17* and *Deuteronomy 5:6–21.* According to *Exodus 31:18,* they were *"written with the finger of God."* The Ten Commandments need to be memorized, but more importantly, applied to our lives. Sometimes, children have a difficult time grasping them. This bracelet and kid-friendly list can serve as great teaching tools.

✞ Marilyn

TEN COMMANDMENTS - Kid-friendly list
1. Do not put anything before God.
2. Do not make fake gods or images.
3. Do not treat God's name badly or use it in vain.
4. Keep the 7th day, Sunday, set apart for God.
5. Give honor to your parents.
6. Do not kill people.
7. Do not treat someone like you are married to them, if you are not.
8. Do not steal things from others.
9. Do not lie about people.
10. Do not wish that you had what belongs to others.

Jewelry Gems

And God spoke all these words, saying: "I am the Lord your God ..."
Exodus 20:1-2a

1. The Ten Commandments are relevant today. Why are the Ten Commandments important to you? _____

_____

_____

_____

_____

_____

_____

2. How can you help children find examples of the Ten Commandments they can apply to life? _____

_____

_____

_____

_____

_____

_____

_____

_____

_____

Charm Bracelet

"And he said to them, Go into all the world and preach the gospel to every creature."
Mark 16:15

Little dangly things hanging from a delicate chain have mesmerized me since childhood. One day my oldest daughter, Theresa, was wearing a beautiful bracelet with many charms. As she told me about each charm, I enjoyed the journey through memory lane with her. Not long after that, I went to the Texas Music Educators' Convention in San Antonio. I discovered a booth with; you guessed it, charm bracelets! I had a blast!!!

There were music charms, Christian charms, jewel charms, etc. I could hardly wait to show Theresa. I knew my duaghter would really like my charms since she is a music teacher, too. Sure enough, we had that special time together and truly enjoyed each other's reactions to the charms.

Since that time, I have been given more charms: Mom, Grandma, cross, Christian fish sign, jewels, etc. Now I have my very own "memory lane" to share with any unsuspecting person I encounter, ha! What a fun and nonchalant way to share the gospel with someone as you draw their attention to the cross charm, fish, or other valuable charms on your bracelet.

Sharing the goodness of God and what each charm represents brings joy to the heart. These simple casual meetings can lead someone to consider receiving Jesus as they experience your passion for God.

Can you imagine how this simple charm bracelet can launch you into a ministry of sharing the gospel? Can it actually connect you to the great commission?

♪Linda

Jewelry Gems

1. What is the great commission according to the Bible? _____

_____
_____
_____
_____

2 Write about a charm that you cherish and explain why you like it.

_____
_____
_____
_____

3. How could you use charms to share the gospel? _____

_____
_____
_____

Yellow Rose

"I am the rose of Sharon, And the Song of lily of the valleys."
Song of Solomon 2:1

A little dainty porcelain yellow rose pin was one of my mom's favorite pieces of jewelry. When she brought out her pins and pendants, I was always drawn to the rose pin.

For my parents' 50th wedding anniversary, we had a cake decorated with yellow roses. There were lots of cut yellow roses all over the room. Mom thought it was the most special day ever.

I remember Mom didn't want presents or cards. Instead, she just wanted people to bring non-perishables for the church's food pantry. That day, family and friends brought an incredible amount of food. This was what my mom was all about, giving and helping people.

Even when she had cancer, I remember Mom sitting in the chemo chair. It wasn't about her, but about others and what they needed.

While getting treatment, Mom shared her testimony. She was always sharing her heart and love for Jesus to individuals that needed to hear all about God's love.

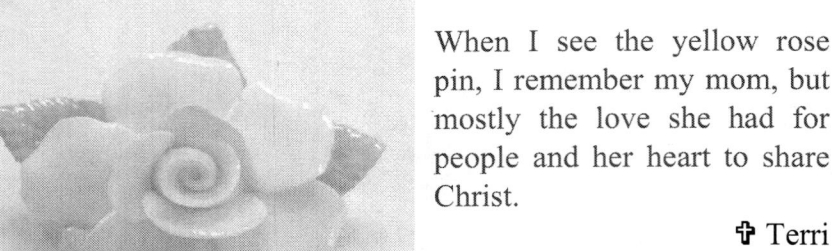

When I see the yellow rose pin, I remember my mom, but mostly the love she had for people and her heart to share Christ.

☦ Terri

Jewelry Gems

With whom can you share Jesus? Write their names here so you can pray for God to prepare their hearts to hear His words through you.

Drama, Drama, Drama

Jesus said, "For I have given you an example, that ye should do as I have done to you."
John 13:15

I am the proud, blessed mother of three beautiful, strong Christian daughters. The oldest, Theresa, is a music teacher and also works with youth through Young Life; Sandra is a music/drama teacher; the youngest, Carolyn, is the administrative assistant to the dean of Tarrant County College. All three are mothers and have blessed me with seven awesome grandchildren. These brilliant and creative ladies kept me on my toes during their younger years at home.

Theresa we called "chatter box." She is 18 months older than her next sister. When it came time for Sandra to learn to talk, Theresa thought it was her job to talk for her. I thought Sandra would never learn to talk!! I had to separate them and give her a chance to say something.

Never in a million years would I have thought that God had a plan for that scenario. Our third daughter arrived on the scene three and one-half years later and was her own person.

Years later, at Oral Roberts University, Sandra became the co-leader of the Charakter Mime Troupe and traveled the U.S. I attribute her ability to remain "mute" for long periods of time to her older sister!!! Ha!

After graduating, Sandra became a drama teacher. It was my joy and pleasure to accompany her to the Texas Educator's Theatre Association where she conducted a mime workshop for drama teachers from all over the state. My daughter was absolutely amazing!

Between workshops, we went to the exhibits. Over to the side I found a booth with drama jewelry. Now, finding that kind of treasure is rare. The drama face earrings absolutely "spoke" to me. They are now in my joyful possession and paraded about on my earlobes for all to marvel over. Just kidding, but they do draw attention. I then have the opportunity to share where I bought them and why I was at the convention. You see, Sandra mimes to Christian story songs, therefore, the avenue to share the gospel is paved.

God uses unusual things, like jewelry, to give us open doors to share His love and His Word with others. What non-conventional jewelry do you have that God has put in your hands for His purpose?

♪Linda

My daughter, Sandra.

Jewelry Gems

1. Describe a piece of unusual jewelry you have._____

_____

_____

_____

2. How can you share the gospel message with it? _____

_____

_____

_____

Witness Bracelets

It is a privilege to be part of the G.A.L.S. We have been given the distinct honor of sharing the love of Jesus to oodles of people in many different places. Often people look for ways they can tell others about God's redeeming love. Our witness bracelets make sharing your faith easy and fun!

Anytime someone comments on the unique design of the bracelet, it's an open invitation to share about the meaning of the colors and shapes of the bracelet. For example in the grocery store, the cashier might comment on the bracelet. With a captive audience, one can share the Word of God in less than five minutes by explaining the colors and significance of each.

✞ God's Amazing Love Storytellers

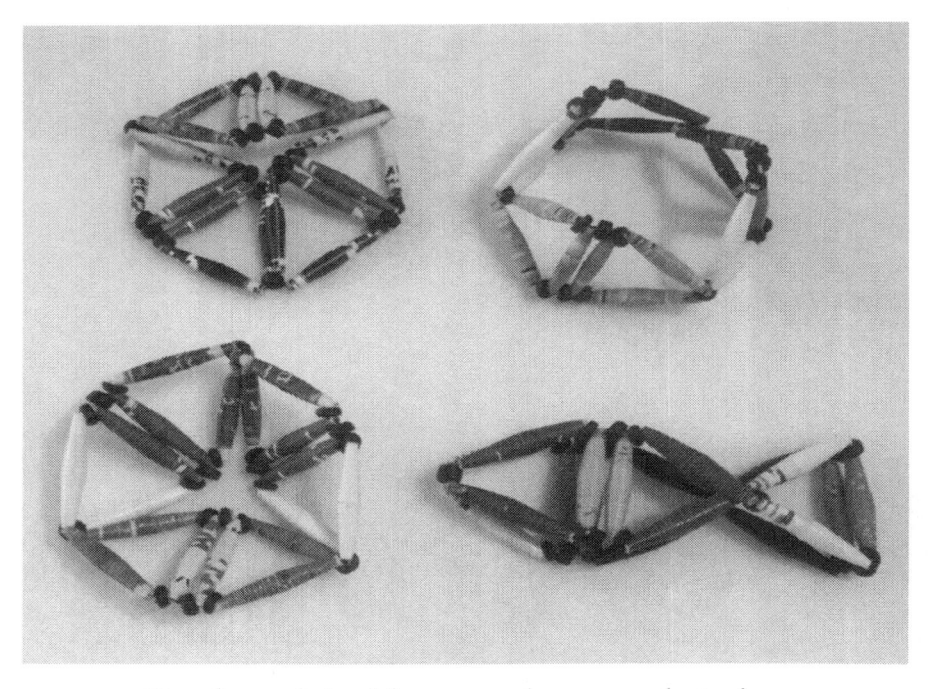

One bracelet with many shapes and stories.

Jewelry Gems

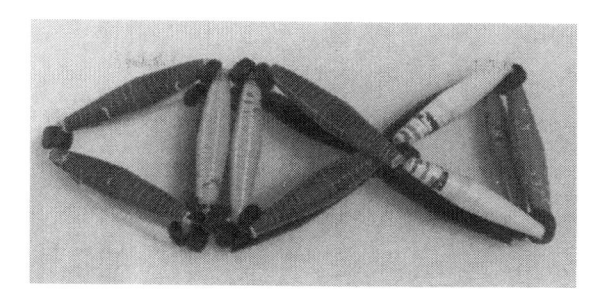

First, the bracelet forms a fish. Many of Jesus' disciples were fisherman. When He asked them to follow Him, Jesus promised He would make them fishers of men. He commanded His followers to also do the same thing. The fish shape compels us to share our faith with others. The symbol of the ichthys, at the bottom, translates in English as "Jesus Christ, Son of God, Savior." Early followers used to draw the shape in sand or dirt so people would know they were followers of Christ. The ichthys and the fish shape show our mission and identity in Christ.

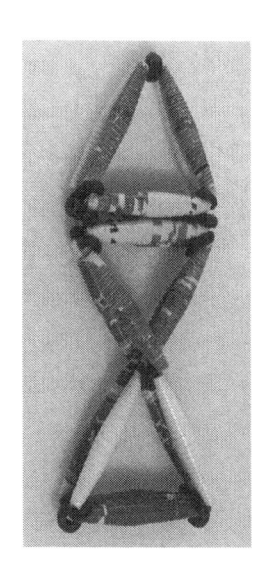

Next, the bracelet turns into a concentric circle which reminds us that when we accept Christ as our Savior, we become part of God's eternal family. Now, we have brothers and sisters in Christ. This is a bond which cannot be broken. It also reminds us of the beauty of the body of Christ. We each have our own special gifts, talents, and roles which are all equally important in the Kingdom of Christ. Others see Christ's body broken for our sins when they look at this shape.

Next, if you squeeze the bottom two edges together, the bracelet becomes a basket which reminds us of the story of the loaves and the fishes that the little boy gave to Jesus when He fed the 5,000. This shape teaches us that God multiplies time, energy, money, and efforts. When we give our "little" to Him, He turns our little into a lot. The basket shape is another reminder that we are commanded by Jesus to "Feed His sheep." We are to use our lives to minister and serve others.

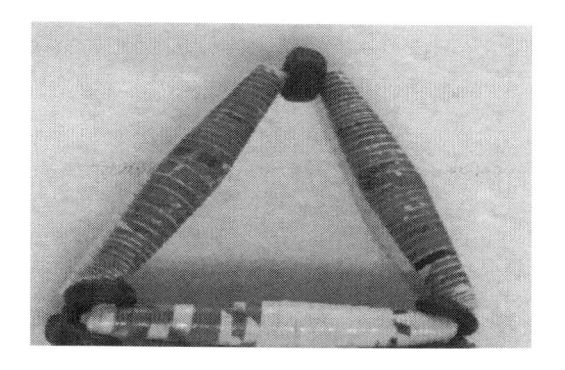

The last shape is that of a triangle which represents the trinity. When someone accepts Christ as their Savior, they also inherit God our Father who was and is the creator of the universe and all things good. We are adopted into God's family. As joint heirs with Christ, we become sons and daughters of the Most High Father God.

The next part of the trinity is Jesus Christ, who was both man and God. He is the Son of the one true Holy God who loved us so much, He doesn't want anyone to perish. Jesus willingly gave His own life as a pardon for our sins through His blood shed on the cross. We can never be "good enough" to enter heaven on our own. God knew that, so He came to us in the form of Jesus to live among us and show us the way to heaven, which is belief in Jesus as our Lord and Savior.

The last part of the trinity is the Holy Spirit. This wonderful gift from God allows His Spirit to live in and through us as we desire to live our life as imitators of Jesus Christ our Lord.

Jewelry Gems

Dark- Represents sin that separates us from God. *Romans 3:23*
Red- Represents Christ's blood shed for us. *John 1:17*
White- Represents cleansing which makes us white as snow.
Isaiah 1:18
Green- Represents growth; Bible, prayer, Fellowship, sharing testimony. *II Peter 3:18*
Yellow- Represents heaven and God's promise that we will live with Him for eternity. *I Peter 1:4*

1. How can you use the colors represented in the bracelet to share your faith with others? Write down what you would say on the spaces below. _____

_____

_____

_____

2. Who can you share the message of the witness bracelet with today? _____

_____

_____

_____

Witness bracelets are purchased from the Philippines and made by widows using recycled paper. The witness bracelets are available at all G.A.L.S. events.

If you are interested in purchasing witness bracelets through the G.A.L.S. please contact us through www.GodsAmazingLoveStorytellers.com.

God's Amazing Love Storytellers

It is our Mission to refresh, entertain, inspire, encourage and lead others to the saving knowledge of Jesus Christ by telling the greatest story ever told of God's Amazing Love.

The G.A.L.S., God's Amazing Love Storytellers, ministry began in Zambia, Africa when Sharon Booker and Carolyn Hedgecock were on a mission trip with Evangelism Partners International in June 2014. During the mission trip, the men were scheduled to help build a church in the afternoons, and Sharon wanted something more suited for the women to do while the men were working. After spending many hours in prayer, Sharon and Carolyn sensed the Lord telling them to share about God's amazing love with women and children in the community. Due to limited resources and suitcase space, they decided to use storytelling as their vehicle because that was also what Jesus did. When they put all the words together, they realized they had an acronym that spelled G.A.L.S.

Once home, the desire to bring God's Word alive through drama grew in both Carolyn and Sharon's hearts. One by one, the Lord connected story tellers through a series of events. Each cast member has unique stories and comes from backgrounds in:

- Education
- Published Authors
- Conference Speakers/Leaders

The G.A.L.S. vision is to share God's amazing stories wherever He leads them to go. No event is too large or too small. Performances include original scripts, music, drama, testimonies, comedy, costumes, dance, and props in Scripture-based presentations which revolve around ways God loves us. Numerous programs are available and can be specifically created for your group or for the needs of your ministry.

For bookings contact:
www.GodsAmazingLoveStorytellers.com.
Email: storytellergals@gmail.com

Writers' Bios and Contact Information

Sharon Booker, a retired educator and her husband John, founded Evangelism Partners International (E.P.I.) in 2009. E.P.I. is a church planting, missionary sending ministry in Zambia and Mozambique. Over one million people have experienced a life change through E.P.I.'s on-going work under the leadership of Coordinator Iwell Phiri. Sharon and John serve as volunteer chaplains at the Tarrant County Corrections Department. They participate in a Good News Club. John and Sharon have two grown daughters and two grandsons. She is co-founder of God's Amazing Love Storytellers and Evangelism Partners International.

Contact her at: www.evangelismpartners.org.

Carolyn Hedgecock is an author, former teacher, script writer, and speaker. Passionate about sharing first-hand experiences of God's amazing love, she and Sharon Booker founded the G.A.L.S. after a mission trip to Zambia. Twice selected Who's Who Among American Teachers, she also received the Outstanding Teacher of the Humanities Award for the state of Texas. Married to her college sweetheart, Joe, she is the mother of a pastor, attorney, and a redeemed prodigal. Blessed with a caboodle of grandchildren, she has no greater joy than to hear All of her children are walking in the truth.

Contact her at: storytellergals@gmail.com

Terri Howell is a survivor of domestic family violence, who understands shattered dreams. She thrills at the opportunity to share the restorative power that God gives! She is a wife, mother of three and "Luvie" to her grandkids. After years of wanting to finish college she realized her dream and received both her Bachelors and her M.B.A. from Dallas Baptist University. Her hobbies include music, crafting, and baking fabulous desserts! She speaks and sings for conferences, retreats, and other women's events. She is an author, Bible study teacher, and is the book advisor/designer for the G.A.L.S.

Contact her at: thowell0604@gmail.com

Linda Patterson, a retired public school music teacher of 30 years, has taught private lessons on guitar and piano/keyboard. She has played on the church worship team over 40 years. Linda has written and directed numerous musicals for school and church. She graduated summa cum laude from Texas Woman's University with a Bachelor of Science in Education degree in Music. *And...I Love You* is her CD featuring spoken healing Scriptures and original songs. The supporting musicians and singers are her family. She has three daughters and seven grandchildren--all musical and artists. Linda is the praise dancer and music leader for G.A.L.S.

Contact her at: jubileefast@yahoo.com.

Marilyn Phillips, a Cum Laude graduate of Texas Woman's University, is a retired elementary teacher and reading specialist. Marilyn has fifteen published books and is a contributor to five different *Chicken Soup for the Soul* books. She has eight book contributions and nine magazine articles published. Marilyn has been married to Nolan since 1972 and they have two grown children. Marilyn is a breast cancer survivor. She praises God for the journey and understands that God is greater than any battle. God's Amazing Love Storytellers has proven beyond any doubt to be a ministry she can share about our great and mighty God.

Contact her at: Mphillipsauthor.com

G.A.L.S.
God's Amazing Love Storytellers

Email: storytellergals@gmail.com
Like us on Facebook @
God's Amazing Love Storytellers Community
Website address:
www.GodsAmazingLoveStorytellers.com

THE JEWELS OF HEAVEN

Have you ever wondered what heaven will look like? Will there be jewels there? John was carried away to heaven in Revelation Chapter 21. Perhaps it is the best description of heaven we have.

Here is what *Revelation 21:10-27 NIV* says:

10 And he carried me away in the Spirit to a mountain great and high, and showed me the Holy City, Jerusalem, coming down out of heaven from God.

11 It shone with the glory of God, and its brilliance was like that of a very precious jewel, like a jasper, clear as crystal.

12 It had a great, high wall with twelve gates, and with twelve angels at the gates. On the gates were written the names of the twelve tribes of Israel.

13 There were three gates on the east, three on the north, three on the south and three on the west.

14 The wall of the city had twelve foundations, and on them were the names of the twelve apostles of the Lamb.

15 The angel who talked with me had a measuring rod of gold to measure the city, its gates and its walls.

16 The city was laid out like a square, as long as it was wide. He measured the city with the rod and found it to be 12,000 stadia [or 1,400 miles!] in length, and as wide and high as it is long [1,400 miles wide and tall!].

17 The angel measured the wall using human measurement, and it was 144 cubits [that is 200 feet!] thick.

18 The wall was made of jasper, and the city of pure gold, as pure as glass.

19 The foundations of the city walls were decorated with every kind of precious stone. The first foundation was jasper, the second sapphire, the third agate, the fourth emerald, 20 the fifth onyx, the sixth ruby, the seventh chrysolite, the eighth beryl, the ninth topaz, the tenth turquoise, the eleventh jacinth, and the twelfth amethyst.

21 The twelve gates were twelve pearls, each gate made of a single pearl. The great street of the city was of gold, as pure as transparent glass.
22 I did not see a temple in the city, because the Lord God Almighty and the Lamb are its temple.
23 The city does not need the sun or the moon to shine on it, for the glory of God gives it light, and the Lamb is its lamp.
24 The nations will walk by its light, and the kings of the earth will bring their splendor into it.
25 On no day will its gates ever be shut, for there will be no night there.
26 The glory and honor of the nations will be brought into it.
27 Nothing impure will ever enter it, nor will anyone who does what is shameful or deceitful, but only those whose names are written in the Lamb's book of life.

Do you want to know how you can enter this majestic place? You can actually find directions for how to get there in the Bible. It's called "The Roman Road."

Find a quiet place and get comfortable. If you have a Bible get yours out and look up the following verses in your version also. Believing that He is Jesus, the Lord and Savior of your life is necessary for you and your family. Take your time; no one is rushing you. Listen to God's voice by being still. Reading God's Word brings calm and assurance to even the most rushed heart.

Here are the simple steps to follow:

1) Acknowledge you are a sinner.

   Romans 3:23, "For all have sinned and fall short of the glory of God."

2) Know all sin leads to death.

   Romans 6:23, "For the wages of sin is death, but the gift of God is eternal life in Christ Jesus our Lord."

3) Understand there is hope and peace through a Savior!

   Romans 6:23b, "But the gift of God is eternal life through Christ Jesus our Lord."

   Romans 5:8, "But God demonstrates His own love towards us, in that while we were still sinners, Christ died for us."

4) Confess your sins to God.

   Romans 10:9, "That if you confess with your mouth the Lord Jesus and believe in your heart that God has raised Him from the dead, you will be saved."

   Romans 10:13, "For, "whoever calls on the name of the Lord shall be saved."

5) Have a relationship with God.

   Romans 5:1, "Therefore, having been justified by faith, we have peace with God through our Lord Jesus Christ."

6) Realize God's promises.

   Romans 8:38-39, "For I am persuaded that neither death nor life, nor angels nor principalities nor powers, nor things present nor things to come, nor height nor depth, nor any other created thing, shall be able to separate us from the love of God which is in Christ Jesus our Lord."

7) Say a simple prayer to God acknowledging your sin. State that you believe Jesus came and paid the penalty for your sins. Because of your faith in God, you know you can be saved and forgiven. Place your trust in Jesus Christ.

This is an example of a prayer that can be prayed:

"Jesus, I do believe You are the Son of God. I believe that You died on the cross to pay the penalty for my sin. I want to live a life which pleases You. I say *"YES"* to Your invitation to come into my life as my Savior and Lord. I want You to be the leader of my life. Thank You for Your free gift of eternal life. I ask this in Jesus' name. Amen."

If you prayed that prayer, you are now part of the family of God, you are a child of His and forgiven. You will spend eternity in heaven.

We want to encourage you to share your decision with someone today. Find a place of worship where the complete Word of God is read and taught.

✞ Remember, God loves you and has a plan for your life!

Did you make a decision to ask Jesus Christ into your life?

Write the date here: _____

Where did this take place? _____

Who can you tell about this decision right away?

_____

If you have questions that may not have been answered about receiving Christ, please contact God's Amazing Love Storytellers, and we will reply to you.

http://www.GodsAmazingLoveStorytellers.com

Our prayer for you is that you know

GOD LOVES YOU!!

Evangelism Partners International (E.P.I.)

God squad on Mission

Sharon and Carolyn Teaching children in Zambia

All gifts are Tax Deductible. Mail Donations to:
Evangelism Partners International
7800 Mockingbird Lane #3
North Richland Hills, TX 76180
or Donate on line @ evangelismpartners.org
Designate: G.A.L.S.O. to contribute to orphanage.
G.A.L.S.O. for Orphans/Widows in Zambia Africa
Contact: http//www.evangelismpartners.org/

In 2010, John and Sharon Booker founded **Evangelism Partners International,** a 501(C)3 (not-for-profit) ministry.

- Over 1,000,000 have heard the gospel and countless thousands have come to faith in Christ.
- For every dollar invested in E.P.I., three people will hear the gospel and two will respond.
- Iwell Phiri is E.P.I. Director in Zambia. He pastors Golgotha Baptist Church. He also trains indigenous pastors, missionaries, and church leaders. In addition, Iwell oversees the current 220 churches, 42 missionaries, and Bible School.
- E.P.I. Zambia/Mozambique is equipped with: one 29 passenger bus, 22 motorcycles, countless bicycles, 24 Solar powered Jesus Film backpacks, SD cards with audio New Testament, Jesus Film and other teaching pieces.
- John and Sharon have provided Scripture sheets and produced small hymnals in the Chichewa and Tumbuka language for new churches. Bibles and hymnals are expensive.
- The king of the region, has donated two pieces of land to E.P.I. Both properties now accommodate churches. The largest acreage has the Training Center. It was constructed by volunteers from 30 surrounding churches with hand-made bricks. The tract will also quarter the G.A.L.S.O. God's Amazing Love Story Orphanage.
- Beginning in 2016, E.P.I. began showing the Jesus Film in Pakistan. Since then over 400 house churches have been started.
- In 2017, God opened the door for E.P.I. to show the Jesus Film and plant churches in Uganda and Tanzania.

G.A.L.S. - Photos

CONFERENCE SPEAKERS/RETREAT LEADERS
DRAMA

PROPS

God's Amazing Love Storytellers

COMEDY

Praise Dance

ORIGINAL SKITS

TESTIMONIES

Sign Language

SCRIPTURE-BASED SCRIPTS

The G.A.L.S. have numerous published books all available on amazon.com. Linda has a CD with original songs.

"Name Game"

Women played exciting roles in the Bible across many centuries. Each had strengths and weaknesses that God used in unique ways. The G.A.L.S. dressed in Biblical costumes presented clues about four lesser known women in the Bible. The audience played the "Name Game" and had opportunities to guess.

MUSIC

Costumes

Patriotic programs will inspire you to celebrate freedom! Contact G.A.L.S. today to schedule an event!

AUDIENCE PARTICIPATION

"Write Your Story on My Heart"

Every day is a blank canvas full of possibility and promise. Jesus wants to take the canvas of our lives with all the hurts, mistakes, and chaos, and turn it into a beautiful masterpiece. The song, "Write Your Story on My Heart" is featured.

Praise Worship

"Believe It or Not"

Do world records have their limits? Is there a point beyond which a record can be broken? The G.A.L.S. and audience attempted to set a new world record. Participates learned some exciting events from the Bible that were truly in the "Believe It or Not" category.

SIGN LANGUAGE

G.A.L.S. use costumes and props for presentations.

TESTIMONIES

G.A.L.S. were on the PRAYER Team for the CMA National Media Summit Content 17

COMEDY **Spiritual truths**

The G.A.L.S. presented to the **Clergy and Police Alliance of Fort Worth** in December.

The G.A.L.S. present at Cornerstone Assistance Network at 3500 Noble Avenue in Fort Worth the first Thursday of each month with a unique and different presentation. Come join us!

"Faith is Timeless"

Faith in God doesn't always make sense; but it makes miracles. Faith is invisible, but it has the power to connect you to what you need. The G.A.L.S. used Biblical costumes as they shared timeless stories how God has remained faithful over the ages. Often, we face the same problems that were encountered during Biblical times.

G.A.L.S.
God's Amazing Love Storytellers

Email: storytellergals@gmail.com

Like us on Facebook @
God's Amazing Love Storytellers
Community

Website address:
www.GodsAmazingLoveStorytellers.com

Made in the USA
Columbia, SC
01 June 2018